P9-DTF-013

CHINESE PORTRAITURE

CHINESE

PORTRAITURE

BY ELI LANCMAN

CHARLES E. TUTTLE COMPANY
Rutland, Vermont   Tokyo, Japan

REPRESENTATIVES

For the Continent:
    BOXERBOOKS, INC., Zurich
For the British Isles:
    PRENTICE-HALL INTERNATIONAL, INC., London
For Australasia:
    PAUL FLESCH & CO., PTY. LTD., Melbourne

Published by the Charles E. Tuttle Co., Inc.
of Rutland, Vermont & Tokyo, Japan
with editorial offices at
Suido 1-chome 2-6, Bunkyo-ku, Tokyo

Copyright in Japan, 1966
by Charles E. Tuttle Co., Inc.
All rights reserved

First Printing, 1966

Library of Congress Catalog Card No. 66-15265

Book design by Simon Virgo
Plate layout by Hide Doki

PRINTED IN JAPAN

To my father
MOSHE LANCMAN

Contents

List of Illustrations

Acknowledgments

It would be impossible to list all those who in one way or another have been of help to me in my study of Chinese portraits. To translate the many volumes of art criticism and history, the work of Chinese scholars during the past fifteen centuries which I used as references, would have taken more than one lifetime; I was therefore forced to draw heavily upon the translations of such prominent scholars as Herbert Giles, Osvald Sirèn and Arthur Waley, to whom I wish to express my indebtedness.

The publication of this book would not have been possible without the kind support of a great number of institutions, museums, temples, and private collectors who have facilitated the study of works in their possession, or supplied me with reproductions from the originals in their collections. As well as those acknowledged in the text, I should like to mention in particular the Bijutsu Kenkyu Institute, the Toyo Bunka, Toyo Bunko, and the Art History Department of the University of Tokyo, who so kindly supplied me with all the necessary material.

Important services have been rendered me by Mr. Simon Virgo who so painstakingly edited the manuscript, and by Miss Yukiko Kimura who diligently typed it. Lastly, I am grateful to my former teacher Mrs. Elise Grilli for stimulating me to research into Chinese portraiture.

ELI LANCMAN

Tokyo

Historical Sources

ALTHOUGH PAINTING is always one of the first manifestations of a developing culture, it is difficult to pinpoint its origins in China—a country whose beginnings are obscure, and clouded by myth and legend. Certainly painting in China began centuries before the earliest works which have survived until today. To find out what happened during the early period we have to rely on description alone—the words of historians and art-critics, catalogs of the imperial collections, and even on legend.

A government department whose function was to collect and preserve outstanding examples of painting and calligraphy was in existence as early as the reign of Emperor Wu Ti (140–87 B.C.) It was at about this time that the mention of portraits in Chinese literature became quite frequent. We know that Emperor Ming Ti (A.D. 57–75) built a special gallery for his collection, and that this example was followed by many of his successors. But the destructive forces of natural calamities, civil unrest, foreign invasion and an unfavorable climate have made the survival of pre-Sung paintings unusual.

Although so many of these early works have been lost, there are some vivid descriptions of them in the large body of art literature that has survived. One of the most important of these critical studies is the ninth century *Li-tai ming-hua chi,* a ten-volume account of Chinese painting from the earliest times to A.D. 841, by Chang Yen-yüan. Another valuable source is the *T'u-hua chien-wen chih,* published in A.D. 1074, which deals particularly with tenth and eleventh century painting.

Catalogs of collections, though, with their biographical and critical notes, are the best source of information. The earliest known was compiled for Emperor T'ai Tsung of the T'ang dynasty, who inherited the art collection of his predecessors of the Sui dynasty. The catalog of Emperor Hui Tsung, published in twenty volumes in A.D. 1120, the *Hsüan-ho-hua-p'u,* is the most important work of its kind, as nearly all of the six thousand works it describes by over two hundred artists were destroyed five years later by the invading Tartars when they sacked Kaifeng.

The famous Imperial Encyclopedia of Calligraphers and Artists, the *P'ei-wen-chai shu-p'u,* is the most complete source up to the end of the Ming dynasty in 1644. It was published in 1708 in a hundred books.

Among the many other basic sources used for this book were the fifth century *Ku-hua-p'in lu,* the sixth century *Hsu-hua p'in,* the *T'ang-ch'ao ming-hua lu*—a survey of T'ang painters published in the tenth century—and the *Wu-lai ming-hua pu'i,* an essay on famous painters of the Five Dynasties.

It is fortunate that although so many works of art have been lost, there is enough literature available for us to get a very good idea of the development of Chinese portrait painting. As Chinese names are so confusing to the Western reader, I hope this introduction makes more clear the context of my sources in Chinese art history.

CHINESE PORTRAITURE

1
The Historical Background

HIGHLY DECORATIVE pottery was made in the valley of the Yellow River at the beginning of the third millenium B.C., by a people who seem to have been Chinese in appearance, but the history of China proper may be said to start at about the sixteenth century B.C.

Its earliest art takes the form of elaborate and formal patterns on bronze vessels. It has been suggested that the foundations of the Chinese bronze culture were worked out in some Central Asian valley and that climate pushed the people concerned eastward, until they settled around the Yellow River. A number of inscribed bones have been recovered from Hsiao t'un in Northern Honan, the capital during the Shang-yin period (18th–12th century B.C.). From these we can tell that early China was a barbaric country controlled by a savage feudal system.

The earliest surviving Chinese pictures are obviously the products of an art long practised. Legend places the origins of Chinese painting at 2700 B.C., and in Chinese literature we find a definite mention of portraiture as early as 1326 B.C. According to native historians, painting came into existence at the same time as writing, and throughout the history of China the two arts are closely connected. (A fine piece of calligraphy is valued as highly as a fine painting, and when a critic evaluates a painting he first looks to see if the brushwork is as personal as the handwriting. In each case the strokes should be full of life—an immediate and direct communication of the artist's mood and thought to his work.)

The feudal system of the Shang-yin period continued through the succeeding Chou dynasty, and at no time was there any centralized government ruling the whole country. Yet the Chou dynasty has always been regarded by the Chinese as the classic age of national culture and been looked to for the pattern of perfection in manners and customs, social institutions, and art. The decorative bronzes of the Shang-yin period were developed further, and it was the age of the great philosophers.

Confucius

The philosopher Confucius, China's most famous son, was born in 551 B.C. during the final stages of the Chou dynasty. He was called K'ung Ch'iu and was later given the honorary title Ta-fu-tsu, whence he came to be called K'ung Fu-tsze. He passed the early part of his life visiting the various courts of China, endeavoring to gain support for his beliefs, but it was not until he settled down in the kingdom of Wei that he was able to perfect his philosophical system, a task which he completed in 495 B.C. He strongly approved of art, not for its own sake but because of its beneficent effect on human nature. Confucius is revered because, single-handed, he did more than generations of his predecessors to consolidate Chinese culture. He did not institute a religion—he formed a code. This code is based on early Chinese rites which were prescribed and legalized during the Chou dynasty.

Importance of tradition

It is these ceremonials which form the basis of the Chinese love of tradition, which is so important in the history of Chinese art. Ever since the remote ages, the rites for family and tribal gatherings had been developing. Founded on the devotion of the people to their rulers and upon the respect of the young for their elders, the state built up for itself a rigid tradition which has lasted to the present day. This ceremonial observance underlies Confucius's great philosophy—a philosophy as sound and as practical as it is remote from the supernatural. Confucius dealt with everyday problems, on the principle that man must set his earthly house in order lest daily problems allow him no time for considering the problems of life and death. His ideal was the "superior man," the

18

gentleman, an essential cog in the complex but efficient machinery of the state. Confucius was an agnostic, and the supreme importance he gave to tradition, order, and rightness ultimately deteriorated amongst his followers into mere respect for age, ceremony, and a good façade. Not to "lose face" became essential, and there emerged an undue conservatism and an irrational insistence on the value of empty form. Thus Confucius, the Superior Man, was unwittingly reponsible for tightening the grip of formalism upon an art already too tightly bound by laws and restrictions.

At almost the same time in the state of Ch'u there lived another man nearly as important in Chinese history—Lao-tzu, the exponent of the doctrine of Taoism. The doctrine that he preached was directly in opposition to that of Confucius, being a mystic philosophy of Nature. *Tao* (the way) is in one aspect the primordial power from which all things in nature have their being. This power was later personified as a divinity in T'ien-tsun, the Lord of Heaven. Lao-tzu's mystic philosophy rapidly degenerated into a widespread code of magical practices and superstitions, and it was in this interpretation of its tenets that its great popularity lay. But at the same time it has always provided a rallying point for liberal poets and thinkers and has inspired much of the best of Chinese painting. Taoism and Confucianism unite in upholding the great domestic cult, the worship of ancestors.

Lao-tzu and Taoism

Not until the third century B.C. did references to painting become at all frequent. At that time the dragon was already a favorite subject, and pictures of animals were common, but for many centuries portraiture remained predominant.

Towards the end of the sixth century B.C. the feudal Chou Empire—which lacked an effective centralised government—began to split up into various small states, and a period of civil war set in. It was at the close of this period, known as "the Warring States" (481–221 B.C.), that there appeared the famous Shih Huang-ti, ruler of the state of Ch'in, who welded all the factions into one empire and ruled as emperor of all China from 221–206 B.C. He established a military state, de-

Shih Huang-ti

The Great Wall

stroyed the Confucian books, abolished feudalism, and left as a monument to himself the Great Wall of China, built at a sacrifice of many lives to keep the invading barbarian tribes out of the country. When he died the country relapsed into disorder, but he had laid the foundations of the Chinese Empire.

Han Dynasty

20 B.C.–A.D. 220

The confusion into which China fell after the death of the dictator Shih Huang-ti did not last long. The house of Han assumed power and from 206 B.C. to A.D. 220 ruled the country, and by means of a far-sighted internal and foreign policy, expanded it into a wide and important empire. The Han rulers succeeded in that most difficult task, the combination after a dictatorship of the best elements of an autocracy with the more moderate views of a representative government. Abroad, the foreign expeditions of the great emperor Wu Ti (140–87 B.C.) and later the campaigns of the great general Pan Ch'ao (*circa* A.D. 73–102) pushed the borders of the empire to India and Persia, and contact was made with the Roman Empire. At home, in the consequent expansion of trade, the rich and peaceful position of the central part of the empire was conducive to the development of the arts.

Expansion of the Empire

For evidence of pictorial art up to the first century of the Christian era we must rely almost entirely on literary allusions. The sculptural reliefs adorning a mausoleum in Shantung, built in A.D. 147, have become famous through their stone rubbings. Of painting as a fine art, however, no trace remains.

We know that painting was widely practiced under the Han Dynasty and can gain some idea of the vanished wall-paintings in the Han palaces from the bas-reliefs which have already been mentioned. It was an art devoted to the service of the state, as was the art of Sassanian Persia and Imperial Rome. The virile stylization of men and animals in highly compact forms is evidence of advanced sophistication without a trace of decadence. Han art may not be as well calculated to impress as that of Rome or Persia, but it is the product of a people with greater sensibility. This can be seen in the frag-ments of actual painting that survive. In Boston, in the British Museum, and in Japan are displayed painted bricks recovered from tombs of the second or early third century A.D. which were opened during the construction of railways in Northern China. The bricks in Boston, which are the best preserved, show courtiers, men and women, watching an animal fight staged in the Imperial garden; the British Museum fragments, which are probably earlier in date, are Taoist in character and show the spirits of the dead being borne to the other world in heavenly cars. Both are summary and not monumental paintings, but they give an idea of the artists' personal attitude to their subjects and of the range of their art. The Taoist pic-tures, behind which lies a faith in magic and occult powers characteristic of the Taoist revival in the second century A.D., succeed in conveying a rare sense of cosmic space and super-natural speed; on the other hand the secular paintings, though they do not quite succeed in expressing a social relationship between the figures represented, are more skillful, more vigo-rous, and more gracefully drawn.

Painted bricks

Six Dynasties
A.D. 220–589

With the fall of the Han dynasty, China was once more split up into several states. The history of China has always followed a pattern—a period of prosperity, which becomes decadent,

21

and then a barbarian invasion of the weakened state, which with its influx of fresh blood revives the failing strength of the nation. Of the various dynasties which came to power during these four centuries, the most important were the T'o-pa Tartars, also known as the Wei Tartars, who ruled over Northern China from A.D. 386–557.

Troubled as these centuries were, they did not pass without significant developments. The most important of these was **Buddhism established** the establishment of Buddhism. Tradition describes its first appearance in China in A.D. 68 with the dream of the emperor Ming Ti, who seeing a golden man fly into the room was advised that it was the Buddha and was converted, but it is uncertain when the first missionary from India actually penetrated into China. By the fourth century, however, when the Chinese were admitted to the priesthood, the religion had really begun to gain power.

Although the names of earlier painters are preserved, Ku K'ai-chih (*circa* A.D. 344) is the first whom we can envisage as a real person. All the early histories of Chinese painting make long references to him, and he is represented in the British Museum by a long silk scroll illustrating "The Admonitions of the Instructress to the Court Ladies," a moral treatise in the form of short passages explaining the painted scenes. Ku K'ai-chih lived at a time when Buddhism was making great progress in China and is known to have painted Buddhist subjects, including a colossal wall-painting of Vimalakirti. It is hard for us, though, to imagine what these can have been like.

A few years later lived the famous painter Lu T'an-wei. He **Lu T'an-wei** is notable for the extraordinary virtuosity of his brushwork, and he is said to have been able to execute a complete drawing with one continuous and rapidly moving stroke of the brush. This mastery over the unbroken line was the twin ideal of both painting and writing, and the parallel development of the two arts was never closer than at this period.

There were many artists hardly less famous in the fifth and sixth centuries, one of whom, Chang Seng-yu, should be mentioned. He was a prolific worker and painted many pictures for Buddhist temples besides the portraits for which he was famous. For him, as for other artists of the day, the dragon and the tiger were creatures which had a special appeal. During two thousand years the popularity of these motifs had been increasing, partly due to the symbolic significance which they shared with the tortoise and the red bird as emblems of the four quarters of the world. But now the tiger and the dragon outstripped their heraldic compeers in public favor, for they began to be imbued with new attributes—the dragon with spiritual forces and the tiger with earthly power.

Tiger and dragon motifs

Sui and T'ang Dynasties
A.D. 581–906

A long time had elapsed since the days of a united China. The country was now united religiously as a Buddhist nation but was still divided politically. It was the Sui dynasty that finally achieved unity, and although it did not hold power for long, its monarchs laid foundations for the T'ang to build on. The Sui rulers actively patronized Buddhism, and this more than anything else seems to have united the nation and prepared a fertile field for a more rapid growth of culture. Buddhism quickly achieved a greater pre-eminence than ever before, and its increased popularity encouraged a tremendous activity among artists and craftsmen. Thousands of new temples were built and decorated with mural paintings, sculpture, banners, and statues of silver and gold. It was to the new spirit of the Sui dynasty that the golden age of the T'ang period owed its inception.

Spread of Buddhism

With the T'ang dynasty China entered into its greatest period of political prosperity. Under the founder of the dynasty T'ai Tsung (A.D. 627–649) and later under Ming Huang (A.D. 713–755) the borders of the empire were extended to India and toward the Caspian sea. With such monks as Hsüan-tsang, who returned in A.D. 645 with a group of copies of famous Indian images, Buddhism attained its greatest period of power and influence—in spite of the adoption of Taoism as the official religion. Just as in other aspects of life, so in painting, it is to the T'ang age that the Chinese have always looked as their period of classic achievement. It is therefore a pity to have so little from which we can form an opinion of the justness of their reputation. Now that many of the pictures which had been attributed for centuries to the T'ang period are attributed by scholars to a more recent date, the number of generally accepted T'ang paintings is extremely small. Two or three scroll-paintings, some Buddhist paintings preserved in Japan, a few other Buddhist paintings on silk, frescoes found at Tun-huang in Chinese Turkestan and other cities in Central Asia, and some objects decorated with landscapes in the Shōsō-in in Japan—these are almost all that we can point to as primary evidence of the T'ang style.

Scarcity of T'ang paintings

But it is when we turn to Buddhist painting that we feel we are approaching the central theme of T'ang art. Partly because of its foreign origin, partly because of its hieratic requirements, but most of all because of its contact with the masses, Buddhist painting in China has followed a course rather apart from the rest. Its most flourishing period was in the first two hundred years of the T'ang period, and the greatest artist of this age was Wu Tao-tzu, a Buddhist painter. He is said to have painted more than three hundred Buddhist frescoes in the palaces of Ch'ang-an and Lo-yang. These perished, along with much of the rest of the great T'ang Buddhist art, during the persecution of the Buddhists between 841 and 845. Nothing now remains of his work. He is said to have used a violent, sweeping style, with draperies blown out as if caught in the wind, however there is no trace of such a violent style in later Buddhist paintings nor in Li Chen's five paintings of patriarchs, carried back to Japan from China by Kōbō Daishi in A.D. 807.

Buddhist painting

The paintings at Tun-huang cover a period of about five hundred years, from the sixth century to the beginning of the eleventh. Within these years the dating of the wall-paintings is a matter of conjecture and some disagreement, but a number of the paintings on silk and paper recovered by Sir Aurel Stein and M. Pelliot are dated and it is possible to place all of these between the years A.D. 729 and 1030. The wall-paintings show the development of the Buddhist style from a simple flat arrangement in narrative bands, through a period of majesty during the early T'ang when the figures have weight and scale but stand in a purely hieratic relation to one another, to the later T'ang period (from the eighth century onwards), when the interest is in the very complex composition.

The greatest landscape painter during the T'ang dynasty was Wang Wei (A.D. 699–759). Only a few paintings with any claim to be his survive (although there are a few paintings and stone-rubbings from engravings attributed to him, among them the *Wang-ch'uan* scroll), but we do know something of his reputation and his career at court. He was the first of the many painters who were also poets. In his poetry he followed classic lines and was not as free or as vigorous as his great contemporaries, Li T'ai-po and Tu Fu. But in painting he was an innovator and was later regarded as the founder of the Southern School of Painting.

Wang Wei

Five Dynasties
and Sung
A.D. 907–1279

After the fall of the T'ang came a period of unrest which lasted for half a century. In this short period five dynasties arose and fell. Conditions were adverse to any continuous development, although there lived two or three painters who have earned the praise of posterity. Early copies of their work show a refinement and delicacy learned from the declining period of late-T'ang art and are prophetic of the perfection of

Unsettled conditions

25

these qualities achieved during the following Sung period.

The Sung dynasty ruled over a China which for the first time was safe to live in. There was time and opportunity to savor the sweetness of life. Culture spread and art and literature flourished. After so much that was material, life moved in the direction of something more spiritual. In the first place, Buddhism underwent a change. The most popular form was the **Philosophy of Ch'an** Ch'an creed, a meditative philosophy practised as an intellectual game of question and answer. The beauty of a pine tree laden with snow, wind in the grass, the flight of a bird across the moon, and the leisure to watch them and to meditate on them were things that attracted the Chinese.

Wang Wei was the first poet-painter of the T'ang period; later almost all artists moved in literary circles, and their interests became increasingly intellectual. Under the influence of Ch'an, their ideal was to live the life of a hermit in scenery of **Tartar invasion** grand desolation. In 1125 the Tartars seized the capital, Kaifeng, and imprisoned the imperial family and court. The northern part of the country was permanently lost and a new capital was established at Hangchow in Chekiang. The earlier part of this period is known as the Northern Sung and the later as the Southern Sung. The Northern Sung period was marked by the development of a landscape school which is perhaps the greatest achievement of Chinese art. Its course was broken at the end by the abortive attempt of the emperor-painter Hui Tsung to induce his Academy painters to study natural objects, instead of imitating only the work of earlier artists. This style gave way after the Tartar invasion to a romantic school of landscape painting which reflected the desire of the exiled artist to forget his exile and hardship by means of communion with nature in its grandest aspects. An art of escape thus succeeded an art of reality.

Landscape is the principal theme of Sung painting, and in its treatment already begins to appear the divergence of what were later known as the Northern and Southern Schools. This terminology, which was first used in the sixteenth century, has little to do with a geographical division or with the two epochs of the Northern and Southern Sung; it is borrowed from a schism in the Ch'an Buddhist sect. The Southern School, which claimed descent from Wang Wei and whose greatest period was under the Northern Sung, was certainly the purer tradition. The artist sought to represent only the essentials of landscape, discarding all trivial and accidental effects. The result was a school of lofty and severe landscape painting such as the Western world has never known. To our eyes there may not seem to be much difference between the paintings of Tung Yuan, Fan K'uan, or the other great Southern School painters and the more romantic emotional art of Ma Yüan and Hsia Kuei. But the Chinese have always tended to reject the method of allusive effect and association of landscape with human emotion which is characteristic of the work of the latter artists. What the Southern School artist tried to do was to set down the object of contemplation in its whole reality and to express in the line the human means of approach to it, so there could be no secondary interest and nothing superfluous in his painting. It is impossible to put into words what he set down in ink or wash, or to describe his paintings without missing their point.

Southern and
Northern Schools

Where there must be such economy of line, a painting either fails or succeeds. We may find the romantic Northern School easier to appreciate because it is not so far removed from Western painting. Difference in technique is not such an obstacle to understanding as difference in purpose. All Western landscape painting is romantic, and its purpose, escape—it is therefore unreal. Chinese landscape painting in the Southern School style is something different and quite new to us. It requires not only loftiness of style but also purity in the artist's life and thought, as well as sensibility and skill in execution.

Although Buddhism no longer occupied the central position that it did under the T'ang, there were still great painters of Buddhist subjects under the Sung. The style of Wu Tao-tzu was still practised, and in addition, in the eleventh century, a new style was introduced by the great painter Li Lung-mien. He was a painter rather than a thinker, and he had great respect for the models of antiquity which he copied. But judging

Li Lung-mien

27

from the paintings either attributed directly to him or known from copies, his style seems to have been severely linear. When he painted in full color, he seems still to have used tone to accentuate his use of line. In character his line was firm and precise rather than free and sweeping, but he was very successful in giving body and weight to his figures, which are monumental in scale. Another aspect of Southern Sung painting **Ch'an painting** was inspired by Ch'an (Zen) Buddhism. Ch'an paintings attempted to reveal truth by a sudden flash of insight, by quick powerful brush strokes and brief telling areas of wash. These are much admired in Japan.

Yüan Dynasty

A.D. 1279–1368

In 1279 the Mongols became masters of China and founded the Yüan dynasty, remaining in power until 1368 when they were driven out and the native Ming dynasty established. Painting continued in the Sung tradition, with certain minor **The Mongol Court** differences. Hunting scenes, in which the Mongols took great pleasure, became a favorite theme. Hundreds of pictures in which horses and horsemen play a part are attributed to Chao Meng-fu, one of the most famous names of the period, but few of these are likely to be originals.

Chao Meng-fu, who was actually a member of the Sung imperial family, was in high favor at the Mongol court. Some of the more independent artists like Ch'ien Hsüan, however, declined to work for the barbarians, and this seems to have caused a loss of initiative which ultimately left Chinese painting so weak that it was unable to take full advantage of the return to a normal national life with the restoration of the Chinese Ming dynasty. The imitation of T'ang subjects did not bring a return of T'ang vitality.

28

The Yüan court was as anxious to preserve Sung culture as it was to use Chinese methods of government. Its conservative outlook influenced the development of the painting schools. During this period, when China formed part of the great Mongol empire, the way was prepared for the complete exclusion of any foreign influence or domestic change.

Insularity of the Yüan

In the meantime the Sung tradition produced great artists. We are fortunate in being able to judge the work of the greatest names in this period by the comparatively large number of existing examples.

Ming Dynasty

A.D. 1368–1644

If no painting had survived from earlier than the fourteenth century, we would rank the Ming dynasty as a great period for art. It has indeed many claims to our admiration, being vigorous and various, and it can boast not only masterpieces of decorative design and rich yet fastidious color, but also splendid ink-paintings, especially in the earlier part of the period. It is only when we have in mind the grandeur of the T'ang style or the lofty mood of Sung that the Ming achievement sinks to a secondary place.

In the sixteenth century two tendencies, both detrimental to good painting, became clearly pronounced. In the first place the worldliness of the court demanded purely decorative paintings. These were executed in a light, minute style, and coloring became brighter. This type of painting is usually associated with the name of Ch'iu Ying, of whose works a great number of copies have found their way to Europe. Ch'iu Ying also seems to have painted in a more literary style. Apart from his figure subjects, there are paintings of birds and flowers in bright colors, or in ink and full colors, by artists

Decorative painting

29

Academic rigidity

like Lü Chi. The second tendency, which affected the more intellectual painters, was towards academic rigidity. This tendency came from the school which during the fifteenth century produced such free and individual works by artists like Shen Chou, Wen Cheng-ming, and Tai Chin. Dispensing with anything but the necessary minimum of line, they produced landscapes in ink which are wonderfully sensitive and suggestive. In the work of Tung Ch'i-ch'ang, however, the regard for the models of antiquity became all-powerful. He was first and foremost a literary man who collected old masters. When he and his fellows took up the brush, they did not make original compositions but took a work by one of the great Sung or Yüan masters of the Southern School as their model.

Early color-prints

To the close of the Ming period belong the earliest known Chinese color-prints—illustrations to a drawing book. The wood-cut was invented by the Chinese long before it was employed in Japan or in Europe. The earliest known example, printed in A.D. 868, was found at Tun-huang by Sir Aurel Stein and is now in the British Museum.

Ch'ing Dynasty

A.D. 1644–1912

In 1644 the Ming dynasty came to an end and the Manchu Tartars, called to help suppress a rebellion, seized their opportunity and became masters of China. The Manchu dynasty lasted until 1912, when the Chinese Republic took its place. This dynasty produced two rulers of supreme quality, Emperor K'ang Hsi (1662–1722) and Emperor Ch'ien Lung (1736–1795). During the long period of their two reigns, China passed through a period of such prosperity that it is hardly surprising that the arts—particularly that of porcelain—should have reached an extremely high standard.

In painting, however, the period did not produce much that was new. Nonetheless, it was by no means lacking in masters of first-rate quality, and the Chinese themselves do not regard it as a period of decline. On the contrary, the Southern School produced four great masters of literary style, known as the "Four Wangs." These masters, who are only artistically related, have the first character of their names in common. They are Wang Shih-min, Wang Chien, Wang Hui, and Wang Yüan-ch'i. According to Arthur Waley, the third of these, Wang Hui, has the greatest reputation in China, but in some circles at least, Wang Yüan-ch'i is preferred. Though equally conservative in their ideas, they were much stronger in execution than the Ming painters. Being confident, they were freer in touch and could indulge in subtleties without losing strength. During this time a new technique known as "bone-less" painting was introduced. It consisted of painting in wash without the use of any line. This was practised by Wang Hui and also by Chu Ta. They set themselves to conceal their skill behind the apparent carelessness of their execution.

The "Four Wangs"

The last of the literary painters whom we need mention is Yün Sho-u-p'ing (or Nan-t'ien), who did for flower-painting what the Four Wangs did for landscape. He was a conservative painter, and literary in his tastes. Disliking the Ming tendency of impressionistic flower-painting, he returned to the realistic art of Sung for his inspiration.

Yün Sho-u-p'ing

All these artists modeled their style on the classic masters of Sung and Yüan. There were, however, a few artists working in newer styles. At the very beginning of the period Ch'en Huang-shou seemed to be showing the way for the development of a baroque school out of the mannerist painting of the day. Others were experimenting in technique and using either a hot stylus or the finger tip. There was also a return to favor of the hunting subjects which had delighted the Mongol conquerors in the Yüan period. One of the most successful artists who catered to this taste at the Manchu court was an Italian Jesuit, Giuseppe Castiglione, who worked for the emperors Yung Cheng and Ch'ien Lung, and received the Chinese name

31

of Lang Shih-ning. He was extremely skillful in combining the European science of perspective and chiaroscuro with the Chinese technique of painting on silk, and he was later to influence the development of Chinese painting along Western lines.

2
Understanding Chinese Portraits

ONE DEFINITION of a portrait is "a record of certain aspects of a particular human being as seen by another." Whether the artist tries to capture the subject's physical appearance, his spirit, or his social position is of little consequence. As long as some sense of the sitter's identity as a particular person remains, the artist will have painted his portrait.

Some critics hold the view that while Western art emphasizes human figures, Chinese art emphasizes landscape painting. As for portraits—such as the ancestral portraits which were so much sought after by Western collectors, who compared them to the works of such sixteenth- and seventeenth-century European painters as Holbein and Frans Hals—these critics believe that if, as such, they do deserve a place in Chinese art, then it is a very insignificant one.

If we consider the history of Chinese art as a whole, this conclusion is clearly far from correct. In the early days before the T'ang period, the chief subject of Chinese painting was the human figure. In the T'ang period, painters began to show a great interest in painting horses as well, while landscapes and pictures of plants and birds reached their height of maturity during the Five Dynasties. In the Northern Sung period landscapes on the one hand and pictures of plants and birds on the other were equally popular with the painters. Through-out the long period from the Southern Sung to the Ch'ing dynasty, landscapes provided the dominant subject-matter for Chinese artists. Throughout all periods of Chinese art, however, from the early days until the fall of the Manchu

Portraiture
in Chinese art

court, portraits were painted in China, and like figure- and landscape-painting, the art of portraiture had its periods of rise and decline, while in the West it was only during the first years of the Renaissance, around A.D. 1400, that the first consistent tradition of portrait painting came into being.

Chinese painting, like the painting of other cultural areas, began with figure painting done for the purpose of keeping a pictorial record of important events, and portraiture occupied an important place in achieving that object. The Chinese artist, unlike those of other early cultures, was not afraid of portraying human figures—indeed, he was ardently devoted to it.

Early figure painting

The first definite mention we have of portraiture is in 1326 B.C., but it is not until the second and third centuries B.C. that these references become frequent. The bas-reliefs found in Han tombs are thought to be engraved copies of paintings the dead man owned during his lifetime.

Figure-painting has been one of the highest art forms in all periods of Chinese art. There has been no attempt to introduce the effects of high-relief or the round-boss of sculpture, nor is there any trace of light and shade—of chiaroscuro. The figures stand, as it were, in a natural light which suffuses them and casts no shadows. From early days, Chinese portraiture—which includes what western art calls figure painting—occupied a preponderant place in Chinese painting.

Creating a living personality has been one of the great achievements of Western painters. There has been no Chinese Titian, Raphael, or Rembrandt because the scholar-painter of China looked down upon the mere representation of physical features and considered professional craftsmen's paintings of ancestral portraits an inferior art. To the Chinese, a portrait is not merely a picture which happens to take as its plastic basis the form of a particular human being. The discovery that a human figure may be treated as impartially as a sack of potatoes was never made by the Chinese. They never disentangled the forms they depicted from the human associations with which these forms were enveloped. They looked upon por-

**Chinese attitude
towards portraiture**

traiture as a composite art, an amalgamation of picture-making and biography. The Chinese held that literal reproduction of the features never fully revealed the character of the subject, but that the painter must use what today would be called "psychological clairvoyance" in order to reveal his subject's soul. Thus, Ku K'ai-chih, the first named Chinese painter, speaks of *chuan-shen,* (showing the soul of the sitter), and to obtain this result, literal representation must often be sacrificed.

"The soul of the sitter"

Consequently, Chinese portraits were never merely a transcription of the features of the subject but rather a composite of what the painter thought the essence of the man to be, founded on his knowledge of his life and lit by his imaginative insight. This theory assumes that man's features and pose do not fully reveal his character, for if they did so, an accurate representation of the body would at the same time depict the inner qualities of mind. The nearest approach to this method in the West is the one we employ in our portrayal of saints.

So little has survived from the great Chinese period of portrait-painting that we are unable to guess the exact stage of development in Chinese portraiture during these years. We can reconstruct and try to understand the essential points through Chinese art criticism and ancient historical volumes. The ancients used only a few outline strokes, yet they could capture the spirit of heroism and elegance: "Ku K'ai-chih added three hairs to the chin to bring out a sense of dignity." Sometimes the spirit of the sitter is centered in one feature, perhaps the mouth or eyes, and sometimes in the skin texture or complexion, and by emphasizing that particular point the artist could bring out the spirit of his subject. The figure was not placed against a background filled with furniture or other objects, nor yet against a landscape, but upon a plain background with nothing to distract from the figure itself. Even the earth on which the subject stood was not sketched in. Yet the Western onlooker is not aware of these deficiencies, so firmly do the figures tread and so powerful is the presentation. Also, in spite of his lack of knowledge of anatomy in the

Simplicity of brushwork

35

western sense, the Chinese artist never failed to give a complete feeling of the body's structure under all its clothes.

The supreme example of such portraits is the one of Li T'ai-po by Liang K'ai, in which the figure seems to walk on air and the tilt of the head suggests an indescribable vitality **Plates 30, 31** of spirit. (See Plates 30 and 31.)

By the end of the tenth century, when landscape-painting had gained popularity, portraiture fell more and more into mechanical hands. During the Yüan period, painters became so interested in physical appearance that they studied the science of physiognomy and applied additional modeling to the face, while the drapery was often rendered in the sketchy brush tradition of the Southern Sung painters.

Portraiture was revived in the sixteenth and seventeenth centuries by the great literary painters, who loved to paint one another in landscapes, fruit-gardens, and other romantic settings. In this case, the spirit was often expressed in the surroundings rather than in the figure, and the background was made to typify the character of the sitter.

The bourgeoisie later imitated this genre, and it became customary for a son to secure a *hsiao-ching* (small view), in which he commemorated the habits of his deceased parents. They were shown in the pursuit of their daily occupations, the father wearing his official robes and attending to his duties and the mother in the kitchen among the pots and kettles.

Religion and art Religion has always been fertile soil for art to spring from. Many of China's so-called gods were men or women who led exemplary lives or bestowed some benefit on their fellow men. Upon them was conferred a posthumous ennoblement, just as the Catholic Church confers sainthood. The function of deities in China, however, was more secular than religious. The power to create gods was in the hands of the Chinese Government, which sponsored and built shrines to honor the men and women who had been deified.

Confucius, like Plato, held that art should serve the state and should kindle and sustain the patriotic virtues. He placed particular emphasis on filial piety. A Chinese child draws this piety in with his first breath, expresses it by service so long as his parents are alive, and by ancestral worship continues it after their death. This teaching fostered the development of portrait-painting, especially of the painting and carving of portraits of great men of the past, in order that they might furnish to each successive generation models worthy of emulation. (One of the earliest references to painting is found in the "Family Sayings of Confucius," in which the sage is described as visiting a palace at Lo-yang, in 517 B.C., where he saw portraits.) The Chinese dotted their country with shrines to the spirits of their dead, whom they have commemorated by innumerable paintings. They portrayed thus sages, poets, great religious teachers, and heroes and heroines.

Influence of Confucianism

From the early records, we also know that it was the custom for the emperor to honor ministers by having portraits painted of them. Such paintings were done upon the walls of halls set aside for that purpose—"halls of fame" as we would call them. This custom caused much political intrigue amongst the courtiers in their desire to have their portrait shown among those honored.

Another common subject for the Chinese painter was scenes from the lives of the romantic women of China. Foremost among them was Yang Kuei-fei—a subject of whom Chinese artists and writers never tire. She had all the charm of Cleopatra, and her influence on the emperor was great. Her story is pictured at every stage—when as a young girl of fourteen the emperor Hsüan Tsung saw her returning from the bath and fell in love with her; when she wore, as the emperor's favorite, "half the robes of an emperor" and reigned in triumph; her tragic death, and the emperor's pathetic search for her even to the gates of Heaven. The empire was ransacked for treasures to lay at her feet, and the great poets Tu Fu and Li T'ai-po and well-known painters such as Han Kan and Wu Tao-tzu worked to please her. Her extravagance finally ruined the country and revolution broke out. The court fled before the outraged populace. There came a day when the starving soldiers who accompanied the emperor in exile de-

Romantic women

manded her life, and in order to save her from a worse fate, the emperor at length yielded and ordered her to be strangled. But even in death she remained beautiful. The emperor abdicated and spent the few remaining years of his life grieving for her.

Court paintings

The depiction of court scenes was the specialty of a succession of painters, the first of whom is said to have been Chang Hsüan, who lived in the eighth century. Unlike Western painters who chose to portray the dramatic moments of a man's life, the Chinese preferred to depict the intimate moments. In portraits of the emperor Ming Huang, for instance, it is his unofficial side that we see—lying at ease, playing the flute, or playing chess. Artists delighted, too, in the portrayal of women—ladies of rank amusing themselves or making their toilet. In the latter case, though, the portrait never shows the woman's body—a subject so admired by western painters; she is always fully-clothed and about to put the finishing touches to her hair and face.

The barbarians

China, from her earliest days, has been surrounded by barbarian hordes ready to sweep down upon her rich country. Sometimes they conquered her, sometimes she held them in subjection, but always their ways intrigued her painters and provided fruitful subjects for their brushes. They portray the barbarian chiefs, their crude customs and manners, their riding, hunting, and tribute-bearing missions to the Chinese emperor. The first great painters of this subject were the brothers Yen Li-te and Yen Li-pen of the T'ang period.

*   *   *

The most important fact that a student of Chinese portraiture must remember is that the actual subject and the features shown in his portrait will seldom be physically alike.

A Chinese portrait painter seldom drew direct from the subject. If a painter portrayed a person who was still alive, as some of the masters did, he would do it from a series of memory studies and would get his impressions from short glances at the subject. His aim was to catch the spirit rather

38

than the form and features. According to a seventeenth-century critic, "to see the spirit of a man is like watching a bird cross your vision. The faster he flies, the greater the spirit, and therefore the briefest glimpse of a person is when you catch the spirit most." The only time when a portrait was painted directly from the subject was when an ancestral portrait was being done, and the Chinese did not consider this an art form.

To our eyes, these ancestral portraits have a special appeal, probably because of their decorative value or their similarity to Western art. Actually, however, most of them achieve nothing more than a representation of characteristic features, many of them assembled from stock types of nose, eyes, mouth, and chin. Only a very small number of them retain something of the indefinable inner spirit which was the aim of the scholar-painters. Ancestral portraits never appeared in art collections in China but instead were considered a part of ancestor worship and treasured solely for that purpose.

Ancestral portraits

Those who could afford to do so procured full-length, highly colored portraits of their parents. These *ta shou,* as they are called, were the only paintings done directly from the model. In some cases they were painted while the subject was still alive, but more often the painter was called in to draw the head after death, during the three days before the burial. The artist made a careful sketch of the face, took notes as to the proper costume in which to show the deceased, and finished the picture at his studio.

The bodies of both men and women were placed stiffly seated, full-face, the feet resting on a teak stool, the hands in the lap. An official was shown in his state robes and cap; a private person wore the ceremonial attire of the father acting as the family's high-priest. The portrait was hung directly over the coffin during the funeral ceremonies and then was carried in the funeral procession so that it could be inhabited by the spirit of the dead during the services. After the burial it was hung up in the private ancestral hall of the family, or in one of the community places, called *tzu t'ang,* which were built for the common use of the families of the same clan. The

Ritual purpose

object of these portraits was to afford a lodging place for the soul, and the soul must not realize that it was being tricked; therefore, an absolutely convincing likeness was necessary. The painter in many instances was compelled to draw the face over and over again until he succeeded in achieving this perfect a likeness. The portrait was thereafter only brought out during the first six days of the year, when all ancestral portraits in the family's possession were hung and reverence paid to them.

The funeral-portrait had a purely ritual purpose. In a few cases it might be a work of art, but the odds were against it. They were seldom painted by a noted artist, but usually by an artisan-painter. One of the few instances when such a portrait was done by a well-known artist was in the year 1050 when Ho Ch'ung, a contemporary of Li Lung-mien, was commissioned to paint a posthumous portrait of a prominent old country baron. Large numbers of eighteenth- and early-**Popularity in** nineteenth-century funeral portraits found their way to Europe **Europe** and soon became popular among collectors. Artistically speaking, however, they are some of the most repulsive paintings in existence.

3
Early Stages

FOR DETAILS OF the development of early Chinese painting we
are forced to rely on Chinese scripts.[1] According to the *P'ei-
wen-chai shu-p'u,* the invention of painting is generally attributed
to Shih Huang, a minister of the legendary Yellow Emperor
who ruled over China more than 4500 years ago. There is no
actual evidence, however, of the existence of such a person
or dynasty. Shih Huang is supposed to have been a contemporary of Ts'ang Hsieh, who first taught the art of tracing the
pictographic script with a style, and so invented Chinese
writing. Most of the anecdotes which refer to painting in early
times tell us about portrait paintings. Regarding the materials
used, though, or the way in which they were executed, no
information is given.[2]

Invention of painting

The first mention of painting in the classics refers to portraits made to honor the imperial ancestors of a ruler of the
Shang-yin dynasty. Reference is made to mural paintings
already existing in public buildings during the Chou dynasty,
among which were many portraits.[3] The decoration of the
interior walls of buildings was one of the earliest roots of
Chinese pictorial art. The annals refer frequently to ancient
emperors who had the audience halls of their palaces covered
with mural paintings which are said to have been similar to
the sculptured bas-reliefs of later times. The " Life of Confucius" describes a visit of the sage in the year 517 B.C. to the
palace of Ching Wang of the Chou dynasty at Lo-yang. It relates
how he saw, on the walls of the audience-hall, portraits of the
ancient Emperors Yao and Shun and of the tyrants Chou and

Wall painting

Chieh, the last degenerate rulers of the Chou and Shang dynasties. Each painting was labeled with words of praise or blame for its subject's virtuous or evil characteristics. On the southern side of the screen, behind the throne, the Duke of Chou was depicted with his infant nephew, Emperor Ch'eng, sitting upon his knee. Returning to his followers, Confucius said, "Here you see how the house of Chou became so great. As we use a bronze mirror to reflect a present-day scene, so antiquity may be pictured as a lesson for posterity."[4]

Confucius and portraiture

In the year 1326 B.C. Emperor Wu Ting of the Yin dynasty had a dream in which God showed him the man who was to prop up his tottering regime. When the King awoke, he described the man's features and ordered a search to be made for him with the aid of a portrait drawn from remembered details. A builder named Yüeh, who answered the description, was appointed Prime Minister.[5]

During the Han dynasty, which followed the Ch'in, there was a marked development of pictorial art in all its branches, as shown by the many quotations in the Encyclopedia* referring to galleries filled with pictures of prominent ministers, generals, scholars, and ladies of the court. Most of the early pictures were painted on the walls of the palaces and temples and have long since perished with the buildings they decorated. We have only literary evidence of their existence, although we do know that they were generally executed by artists attached to the palace.

Former Han dynasty

With the opening of the Former Han dynasty in 206 B.C. we begin to feel ourselves on genuinely historical ground. Despite the ever-present elements of fable in which the Chinese take such keen delight, there is no reason why we should not accept the literary descriptions of the time, many of which have been vividly translated by Professor Giles. For the artistic achievements of the later part of the Han period we have the support of excavated tomb paintings and bas-reliefs.

In the official history of the period is told the story of the

* The *P'ei-wen-chai shu-p'u.*

escape in 202 B.C. of the founder of the dynasty from the city
in which he was besieged by the army of the Hsiung-nu
(the ancestors of the Huns who, until their destruction in the
first century B.C., threatened the northern borders of the Han
state). A clever minister who was sharing the siege sent to the
wife of the Hun chieftain the portrait of a lovely girl, saying
that the emperor wished to offer the young lady as a present
to her husband. The chieftain's wife said nothing about the
picture, but convinced her husband that the emperor was
ruling by the grace of God and that, even if they captured the
city, they could not hold it for long. She persuaded her husband to open a way through his lines and let the emperor
escape.[6]

The Hsiung-nu

Towards the close of the second century B.C., the emperor
ordered a portrait to be painted of the deceased mother of
his most faithful minister, to be hung with other pictures in
the palace of Kan-ch'üan. We are told that the son never
passed this picture without prostrating himself before it in
tears. There also was hung the portrait of Li Fu-jen, the
favorite of the emperor Wu Ti (140–87 B.C.) whose beauty was
such that "one glance of hers would destroy a city, two
glances a state."

The Han annals refer to some interesting portraits among
other historical paintings: "During the reign of Emperor
Yüan Ti of the Former Han dynasty, in the third year of the
Kan Lu epoch (51 B.C.), the Shan-yü or Zenghi of the Hsiung-
nu for the first time in history submitted himself as a vassal
to the Chinese court. The emperor, admiring the magnificent
frame of the warrior, had his picture painted in the Unicorn
Pavilion of the palace. It was an artistic likeness of his form
and features, and was labeled with his rank and dignities as
well as his tribal and personal names."[7] In gratitude to the
warriors and statesmen who had brought about the submission
of the Hsiung-nu, the emperor caused the portraits of eleven
of the most eminent of them to be hung in the Unicorn Pavilion with their names and titles attached.

During the following reign, when western tribes from Tibet

were threatening the frontiers of China, Emperor Ch'eng Ti ordered Yang Hsiung, the great philosopher and statesman, to pronounce a eulogy before the pictures of the dead heroes in the hope that their spirits might come to the rescue of the empire they had once served so well.[8]

In what we may call the Art section of the History of the Former Han, some fifteen or sixteen illustrated works are mentioned, among them "Portraits of Confucius and His Disciples," but as in the case of the many pictures mentioned above, no artists' names are given. Among the six artists whose names have been recorded under the Early Han dynasty

Mao Yen-shou

is Mao Yen-shou, a noted painter of portraits "with likeness guaranteed" whose tragic end is told in the following story. Emperor Yüan Ti (75–32 B.C.) had so many concubines in his harem that he did not know them all by sight. He therefore commissioned the painter Mao Yen-shou to paint their portraits and favored them accordingly. In order to secure pleasing likenesses, all the ladies except Chao-chün bribed the painter—consequently the results of Chao-chün's portrait were disastrous and she never saw the emperor. Later on, when the Hsiung-nu chieftain came for his second audience in 33 B.C., it became necessary to present him with a bride from the imperial seraglio. The emperor, who did not want to give away any of his favorites, chose Chao-chün because of her ugliness in the portrait. He saw her only when it was too late, when she came for farewell audience, and at once fell deeply in love with her. He sent a camel laden with gold to negotiate her repurchase, but the Khan refused to part from such a beauty. The emperor brought Mao Yen-shou to trial, and the painter was executed in the market place the same day.

When Chao-chün died a few years afterwards, the Khan refused to allow her body to be taken back to China for burial. This story (which was recorded in the *P'ei-wen-chai shu-p'u*) later became the subject of a Chinese tragedy which was translated by Sir John Davis and called *The Sorrows of Han*.[9]

The Later Han dynasty began in the twenty-fifth year of the Christian era. The two Han dynasties really form one long

44

dynasty of four hundred years, broken for a few years by the usurper Wang Mang who ruled from A.D. 8–25 under the Hsin dynasty. But the division into Former and Later Han is always made by the Chinese and the two periods may be roughly fixed in the memory as covering two hundred years before Christ and two hundred years after respectively.

During his short reign, Wang Mang sponsored the painting of portraits. He had the portrait of a noble whom he feared painted on the wall of every government office throughout the empire as a warning to all virtuous people. In a work published towards the close of the dynasty, we first read of Shen Shu and Yü Lü, whose names or grim figures are to this day painted on front doors in China to keep away evil spirits.

The Hsin dynasty

Paintings are mentioned under " Chariots and Robes" in the Dynastic History. No list of pictures is given, nor are there any critical notices upon the development of art, but a great deal of information is given about the use of colors in portrait painting. According to one writer, when the old masters painted human figures, they used four colors interchangeably for the upper and lower robes—yellow, white, blue, and purple. They did not use green, for that resembled the color of the dress worn by the common people. For a person playing the lute, either purple or yellow would be used; no other color was possible." Altogether we find the names of nine painters recorded as belonging to this period, among them the great scholar and statesman Ts'ai Yung (A.D. 133–192). He was commissioned by Emperor Ling Ti to paint a picture of the five contemporary generations of a certain noble family, to compose a panegyric upon the fact, and to write it out himself; the results were known as the "Three Beauties," a beautiful, composition, beautiful writing, and a beautiful painting. He also painted for the Hung-tu College the portraits of Confucius and his seventy-two disciples.[11]

Colors used in painting

Under this dynasty we meet with an ever-increasing number of high officials whose portraits were painted by imperial command. This practice, however, had been carried to a ridiculous extent already under Emperor Hsüan Ti of the Former

45

The Imperial Gallery

Han. "Any man," says the philosopher Wang Ch'ung (A.D. 27–97) "whose portrait did not hang in the Imperial Gallery was held by his sons and grandsons to be of small account." In another place the same writer says, "Men love looking at portraits because the portraits are pictures of the dead, and to look upon a dead man's face is, as it were, to hear his words and see his actions. But the writings of the ancients handed down on bamboo and silk will bring about the same results; why confine ourselves to looking at pictures on a wall?"[12]

In the History of the Later Han Dynasty we are also told that in A.D. 61 Emperor Ming Ti (A.D. 57–75) sent a minister to India to obtain information about the religion of Buddha, which had been imperfectly known to the Chinese for some centuries. In A.D. 67 the Chinese mission returned with the Buddhist priest Kashiapmadunga—who died soon afterwards in the capital—and with a number of Buddhist pictures and images. Buddhist influence, however, began to be felt in China at a much later period. The same emperor also had the portraits of sixty officials of merit painted and hung in a gallery of the palace.[13]

Chang Yen-yüan, the well known art-historian of the ninth century, describes in the *Li-tai ming-hua chi* some of the traditional views on portraiture and gives a short account of the early development of painting. He then explains more advanced forms of figure painting dating from the Han period. He writes that the paintings of loyal and filial men which decorated the pavilion on the Cloud Terrace (built by Emperor Ming Ti), and those of brave and meritorious officials in the Unicorn Pavilion (erected by rulers of the Former Han dynasty), were all painted with a moral purpose, because "to contemplate good serves to warn against evil, and the sight of evil serves to make men long for wisdom." He quotes two prominent early authors, Lu Chi (A.D. 261–303) and Ts'ao Chin (A.D. 192–232), in support of the view of painting as a moral force. Ts'ao Chih writes: "When one sees pictures of the 'Three Kings and the Five Emperors' one cannot but look at them with respect and veneration, and when one sees pictures

Moral purpose
of portraits

46

of the 'San Chi' (the last degenerate rulers of the Hsia, Shang, and Chou dynasties) one cannot but feel sad. When one sees pictures of rebels and usurpers of the throne, one cannot but gnash one's teeth. When one sees pictures of great sages and men of high principles, one cannot but forget one's meals." From this we may realize that portrait painting and painting in general served as moral examples or mirrors of conduct. Chang Yen-yüan does not offer any closer descriptions of these pictures, but from his other comments it seems evident that he was referring to wall-painting executed on a plaster surface.

We are still a long way from the time of painters whose works have survived to the present day. Happily, however, we are able to glimpse some of the features of Chinese architectural decoration in the historical records, and a few early examples of portraiture can be seen in the remains of tombs. It was the custom at the time to build large tombs for the dead and to decorate them with bas-reliefs and wall paintings. A great number of these are known; the decorations are executed in various methods, some of them engraved, others more like flat reliefs. Some of them represent fantastic beings of quasi-human and animal shape; others show characteristic aspects of social life in the Han period, such as people at their daily tasks, playing music, and feasting; yet others concentrate on human figures. All figures are shown in profile, and include the name and title of the subject, suggesting that the artist was trying to portray a particular person.[14] An example of this is the stone relief which shows a seated woman (Plate 1). The inscription reads "The filial daughter-in-law Lady Chao, whose style name is Yi-wen."

How far these stone engravings may be accepted as representative of the development of portraiture is not sure. There is no attempt to imitate painting, yet it is evident that the engravings could only have been designed by a painter, for the means of expression is almost exclusively line and the forms are conveyed by the contours. With what fidelity the painters' designs were transposed on to stone, however, is

Decoration of tombs

Plate 1

47

yet a question to be answered. This much is sure, though : the ink-rubbing copies of these portraits are evidence of the mastery of sensitive brush-work in early times. The portraits of

Plate 2

men engraved on stone (Plate 2) show a precision and delicacy of line through which every essential detail is expressed. The softness and volume of the drapery is remarkable.

In 1953 a tomb of the Later Han period was uncovered near Wang-tu, Hopei Province. The inside wall of this tomb is divided horizontally in two, the lower half a series of paintings of animals and birds, and the upper half rows of twenty-four figures—somewhat under life size—whose rank is stated in

Plate 3

the accompanying inscriptions (Plate 3). The idea seems to have been to illustrate how large a number of subordinate officials are saluting or paying homage to a landlord or governor. All the figures are turned in full or three-quarter profile, with strongly individual faces, and are mostly slightly stooped, saluting with joined hands, and in some cases holding a Kuei tablet. The paintings are executed on the thin white coating which covers the trimmed stone walls. The colors are darkened by age and dirt but the broad black outlines have retained their vigorous sweep. Figures like these may serve to give some idea of the monumental wall paintings of the Han period of which so little survives.[15]

We know that even painting on smaller objects of lacquer and clay was not limited to mere decorative design and animal figures. During an excavation at Lo-lang, Korea in October 1931, a small covered bamboo basket decorated with exquisite paintings in lacquer was unearthed with other valuable relics. On every side and edge of the cover and basket are sitting and standing figures, numbering ninety-four in all

Plate 4

(Plate 4). Framing or supplementing these figures are lozenges and *vin rinceau* designs. On the upper part of the basket body, the part which fits into the cover, a frieze of figures forms a broad belt. On one of the two long side strips are ten figures, beginning with the filial son Ting Lan and the wooden image of his father. On the long strip on the other side of the box are ten more figures, among them Wei T'ang. On one of the

1

LADY CHAO. Artist unknown. Later Han. Rubbing of Stone low-relief. Height 87 cm. *(Szechwan Provincial Museum.)*

2

TOMB PORTRAIT. Artist unknown. Later Han. Rubbing of Stone low-relief from Shantung.

3 SALUTING OFFICIALS. Artist unknown. Later Han. Wall painting from Wang-tu, Hopei. Height 236 cm.

4 EXAMPLES OF FILIAL PIETY. Artist unknown. Later Han. Lacquer-
painting on basket found at Lo-lang, Korea. Height 7½ cm. *(National
Museum of Korea.)*

The Lo-lang basket

end strips are the Four Greybeards of Mount Shang and another figure, making five in all. At the other end are five more figures, two of which may represent Po I and the wicked Emperor Chou of the Yin dynasty. All of these are seated figures. On the central sash of the cover there are six figures, among them Emperor Huang Ti—the "Yellow Emperor" of the Yin dynasty—and along the top edge of the cover on all four sides there are rows of small figures, all untitled, numbering forty-two in all. These figures are all in sitting positions. On the four corners of the body of the basket are Emperor Wei-Wang and his queen, the king of Wu, and two pretty women. On each of the four corners of the cover is a standing figure.

Except for the small figures on the edges of the cover, the name of each personage is written to one side. We may suppose that the subjects were taken from the then extremely popular book *Tales of Filial Children*, and from other historical and traditional sources. It is surprising that, whereas the outlines of the hands and faces are done with smooth and flowing lines as fine as hairs, the outlines of the folds in the robes are handled boldly with thick strokes. The heads of the figures are disproportionately large and the bodies short and fat, reminding us of the figures in Yen Li-pen's later period scroll of the emperors. The eyes of each figure are turned far to the right or the left so that the subjects seem to be talking among themselves. According to the inscriptions, there are both elevating and depressing examples of human behavior among the portraits on the basket. The faces of the old people are clearly distinguished from those of the young, but there does not seem to be much difference between those of the men and the women. Since these lacquer paintings are not the work of a noted painter, we can only imagine the beauty of the work of the famous artists of that age, for there is nothing left from their work but descriptions in Chinese literature. It is also clear that the basket must have been brought to Lo-lang from the central part of China by the person who was buried in the tomb.[16]

4
The
Classical Period

With the opening of the Chin dynasty (A.D. 265–420), the artistic horizon begins to widen. Some twenty-two names of painters from that period have been handed down. Only a few of them, however, are recorded as portrait painters. Mention must be made of Wei Hsieh because he is said by Hsieh Ho to have been "the first artist to paint in detail, ancient pictures up to his date having been sketchy."* He excelled in Taoist and Buddhist subjects but painted portraits of distinguished women as well as mythological and historical pictures.

Wei Hsieh

Another on the list is Wang Hsi-chih (A.D. 321–379), who was primarily known as a calligrapher. His paintings were of great merit, and it is said that he painted his own portrait with the help of a looking glass. On the Imperial list we find the name of Wei Hsieh, a pupil of Ts'ao Pu-hsing of the previous Three Kingdoms period. We are told that the figures he painted were so instinct with life that he dared not put the final touch of dotting in the pupils of their eyes lest they rise from the canvas. He excelled in historical portraits and in the representation of Taoist and Buddhist divinities.[1]

We now come to a painter who, to judge from all that has been written about him, both in truth and fiction must have been a great portrait painter. Ku K'ai-chih (A.D. 344–406).[2] If our knowledge about earlier artists and their works is obscure, this is hardly the case with Ku K'ai-chih. Apart from his

Ku K'ai-chi

* *Ku hua-p'in lu,* written by Hsieh Ho at the end of the fifth century.

53

personal characteristics, which have been transmitted to us in historical records, we can, to some extent, observe his artistic ideals in copies or imitations of his paintings. He was a native of Wu-hsi, near the present Nanking, and was famous for his scholarship as well as for his pre-eminent artistic prowess. His range was wide and comprehensive, including portraits of emperors, statesmen, and ladies of the court. From the following stories we get the impression that as a portrait painter he was unsurpassed.

Fame as a portrait painter

"He was once attracted by a girl who lived near, but she would have nothing to do with him. So he painted her portrait on the wall and stuck a thorn in it where the heart would be, and the girl at once began to feel a stabbing pain in her heart. Ku again made advances to her, and this time she yielded. He then removed the thorn from her portrait and the pain ceased."[3] "When he painted the portrait of P'ei K'ai (a prominent scholar) he added three hairs on the jaw, which made the beholder feel very strongly the sagacious character of the man."

"When he painted the portrait of Hsieh K'un (a scholar and musician) he placed him among jutting crags. Someone asked him why he had done so, and he explained that Hsieh himself once said that among hills and valleys he showed to greater advantage so he thought it best to put the fellow among his hills and dales."[4]

He wanted to make a portrait of Yin Chung-k'an, but as Yin had a disease of the eyes, he refused, saying, "I am too ugly; it would not be worth while." Ku K'ai-chih insisted however and replied, "It is just on account of your eyes that you should be painted. Would it not be most exquisite if the pupils were first painted bright and then touched over with a thin film of white, so that they may look like the sun when it is covered by light clouds."[5]

Hsieh An, a well-known statesman and art-lover of the time, valued Ku K'ai-chih's art highly and remarked, "There has never been anything like this since the birth of man." When painting portraits, he often waited several years before putting in the pupils of the eyes. When someone asked him the reason for this, he replied, "It is true that the beauty of frame and limb can be expressed independently of these delicate parts, but delicacy of character depends entirely on them."[6]

The only surviving works which to some extent may serve as support for Ku K'ai-chih's artistic genius are the hand-scrolls known as "The Nymph of the Lo River" and the "Admonitions of the Instructress of the Palace Ladies." There, on a small scale, one may obtain a hint of the possibilities of portraiture in line alone.

Ku K'ai-chih excelled in painting with colors, mainly red and green. The material generally used at that time for water-color pictures was silk. In a treatise on painting Ku K'ai-chih describes the care he always took in selecting cloth for his own use.[7] It had to be of an evenly woven texture that would not warp even when 75 cm. wide. When finished, the picture was pasted on thick paper with borders of brocade and mounted at the ends with rollers of wood tipped with metal, and when rolled up, it was tied round with silk cords fastened with tags of jade or ivory. The usual form was the *chüan* (or *makimono* in Japanese), ranging in length from 30 cm. to 12 meters or more. It was laid horizontally on the table and painted with one or several scenes, space being left at the ends for seals, inscriptions, and critical appreciations. A second form was the hanging scroll (the Japanese *kakemono*), generally shorter and painted vertically. The folding screen has been in use as long as the scroll, but it was not popular during all periods and is much more difficult to preserve.

Scroll materials

Bamboo cut into lengths of about 30 cm. and split length-wise into tablets was probably the earliest writing surface. It was incised with a bronze style or painted with a reed pen dipped in black lacquer. The traditional date of the Chinese invention of paper is A.D. 105, and paper manuscripts from the second century A.D. have been found by Sir Aurel Stein in Central Asia. The invention of the brush is attributed in Chinese literature to Meng T'ien, who died in 209 B.C., but in fact he only contributed to its improvement. Remnants of

Invention of paper and the brush

55

brush writing on oracle bones prove that it was already in existence in the Shang-yin period (second millennium B.C.)

Lu T'an-wei

Lu T'an-wei was the most distinguished artist of the Liu Sung dynasty (A.D. 420–478). He excelled in portraiture and was attached to the court, where he painted emperors, princes, and other famous people of the time. The *Hsüan-ho hua-p'u,* written in the twelfth century, describes him as singularly proficient in all the six canons of art, classes him as a painter of Taoist and Buddhist subjects, and gives a list of the titles of ten of his pictures which were then in the palace. Among them is the portrait of Wang Hsi-chih (the calligrapher of the Eastern Chin dynasty).

Lu T'an-wei's contemporary, Hsieh Ho of the Southern Ch'i dynasty (A.D. 478–502), owes his reputation not to his art but to an essay on painting, the most frequently quoted work in all Chinese art literature. In his *Ku-hua-p'in lu* (Classification of Old Painting) he established six principles intended to serve as standards for the evaluation of pictures.

Hsieh Ho's Six Principles

He is also known to have been a clever portrait painter who required no sittings but after a glance at his subject could go home and "reproduce from memory form, expression, and hair on face and head without fault of any kind." He is said to have introduced a greater minuteness of detail than had hitherto been attained. Huang Po-ssu, the art critic, has the following note on a work by this artist: "The picture of Emperor Ming Ti of the Eastern Chin dynasty (A.D. 322–326) riding in his wheeled chair was painted by Hsieh Ho of the Southern Ch'i dynasty. Although this is only a copy which has been handed down, the conception and likeness are those of ancient times, but to place a small table on the chair and to display two carrying-poles alongside is not at all in accordance with tradition. . . Further, at the time of the Eastern Chin dynasty (A.D. 317–420), hats and boots had not come into general fashion. Yet in this picture, we see the eunuchs wearing them." It is also stated that after the year 501 he failed to catch the likeness and that "the portrait and the sitter bore no resemblance to one another."[9]

With the accession of the Liang dynasty in Nanking (A.D. 502–557) new encouragement was given to letters and the arts. One of the most memorable and important events in the religious history of China happened at that time—the arrival in about 520 of the Indian patriarch Bodhidharma, known in Chinese as Ta-mo. He gave the impulse to a trend of thought and an attitude towards nature and art which in later times bore rich fruits in the field of painting. The teaching of Bodhidharma, to quote Sir Charles Eliot, "imported a special tone and character to a great part of Far Eastern Buddhism." In China it became known as Ch'an, and in Japan as Zen (Sk. Dhyana).*

Bodhidharma and Ch'an

The reign of Wu Ti of the Liang dynasty (A.D. 502–549) was made illustrious by Chang Seng-yu (*circa* 500–520) who was attached to the court and painted many pictures for the Buddhist temples founded by the monarch. Although his name is absent from the short imperial list of names, he ranks by general consent among the early masters. He was eclectic in his sympathies and once painted in the "arbonvitae hall" of an old temple at Nanking a figure of Locanā Buddha in company with Confucius and the ten sages of the Confucian school. When the emperor, astonished, asked him why he had painted Confucius and the sages inside the gates of a Buddhist temple, he replied "They will be of service later." Four centuries afterwards, when the Later Chou dynasty proscribed Buddhism and destroyed every monastery and pagoda in the kingdom, this was the only temple spared, on account of its Confucian frescoes. Chang Seng-yu painted portraits of some princes which are said to have been astonishingly lifelike; unfortunately, none of them is known to have survived. However, a picture which contains characteristic examples of his figure drawing and comparatively strong sense of realism is the scroll known as "The Five Planets and Twenty-eight Constellations." Even though this is a copy made during the eleventh or twelfth century and can hardly be said to possess the

Chang Seng-yu

* It is often said that the real founder of the Ch'an sect was the Chinese priest Hui-neng (died A.D. 713).

individual character and expressiveness that one would expect in orginal works of the sixth century, it exhibits two innovations made by Chang Seng-yu, probably as a result of western influence—the technique of shading and an increased corporality in the figures. In this scroll, which represents all the Five Sacred Planets as symbolic animals with significant attributes, the third planet, Saturn (Chen-hsing, or "the star which wards off evil influences") is represented by a bearded old man, probably an Indian, seated cross-legged on the back of a large bull (Plate 5).

Plate 5

The man looks very much like an Indian Arhat, particularly as he is lifting his right hand in a gesture which in Buddhist iconography indicates absence of fear. This painting supports the ninth-century writer, who summed up the great portrait painters thus: "Ku K'ai-chih captured the spirit of his subjects, Lu T'an-wei (of the fifth century) their bones, and Chang Seng-yu their flesh."[10]

Yüan Ti, a later emperor of the Liang dynasty, was himself an artist. While still a governor of Chingchou, before he came to the throne, he painted the portraits of the "tribute bearers" —foreigners who visited the Chinese court; thirty-five foreign nations were represented in succession (Plate 6). This subject has occupied many painters in China since that time.[11] Yüan Ti's paintings were very popular with Sung and Ch'ing dynasty copyists. Only thirteen of the scrolls of thirty-five portraits copied during the Sung dynasty are known to exist today.

Plate 6

The almost complete destruction of the paintings of the great masters of the pre-T'ang era makes it hard for us to evaluate the achievements of the masters of the time.[12] Owing to the discovery of tomb wall-paintings, however, it is possible to form some opinion on painting, particularly portraits. Tomb paintings usually portrayed the dead man and his family and scenes from his life.[13]

There still exist in Korea several tomb-paintings of this period. They were discovered by Japanese archaeologists in 1905.[14] Typical is the "Tomb of the Four Gods"—probably the persons for whom the tomb was built—near the mouth

5   SATURN. Attributed to Chang Seng-yu. Six Dynasties (Liang). Color
and ink on silk. Height 23 cm. *(Osaka Museum.)*

6 TRIBUTE BEARERS. By Emperor Yüan Ti (copied during Sung period.) Six Dynasties (Liang). Color and ink on silk. *(Nanking Museum.)*

7 WOMAN MUSICIAN. Artist unknown. T'ang, 708 A.D. Wall-painting in tomb near Ch'ang-an.

Plate 7

of the Taedong river in North Korea. Slightly later in period, but containing good examples of pre-T'ang wall-paintings, is the tomb of Emperor Hsüan Tsung's brothers-in-law, which was excavated near Ch'ang-an in 1959. In it was found the portrait of a woman musician (Plate 7). The painting is executed with strong brush strokes and enhanced with green and red pigments. It is among the best examples of tomb-paintings extant in China.

Under the Sui dynasty (581–618), when the empire was reunited with the capital at Ch'ang-an, painters became more numerous. This period is distinguished by three artists, two of whom—Tung Po-jen and Chan Tzu-ch'ien—arrived together at the capital, the one from Hopei and the other from Chekiang. Both of them were given appointments at court, and they both painted portraits which had "breathtaking expressiveness"; apart, however, from historical references to their ability as portrait painters, we have no other clue to their individual styles.[15]

The painter Cheng Fa-shih is known to have studied the works of Chang Seng-yu and become a great portrait painter. Among his better-known pictures were a portrait of Asoka, the Indian king of the third century B.C., and Wen Ti, the founder of the Sui dynasty. "His," says one authority, "was the only footprint since Chang Seng-yu." He painted accessories such as hat-tassels and belts in a most beautiful manner, but his real ability lay in the way he could bring out the individuality of each person he painted.

T'ang dynasty

The T'ang dynasty (618–906) is inseparably associated in the minds of the Chinese with poetry, painting, and music. Li Shih-min, China's man of destiny who became the emperor T'ai Tsung (627–649), laid the foundation not only for a great political organization that lasted for about three centuries but also for a cultural development of wider scope than ever before. From the T'ang era, the names of some three hundred painters have come down to us. There is no lack of artists who attained fame by painting portraits of emperors and dukes, and gay ladies. Very few of the original paintings,

62

which were done on paper or silk, remain today, and again we are obliged to rely on copies and literary records to obtain an idea of certain masters in this field. Yet in spite of the insufficiency of the material, we can see a definite figure-and-portrait style which dominated the pictorial art of China to a degree unequalled before or since.

Passing over several imperial princes, we come upon the painters Yen Li-te and Wu Tao-tzu, named in the imperial list of K'ang Hsi as representative artists of this dynasty. Yen Li-te, who was especially noted for his pictures of "the people of strange countries," was a high official at the court of Emperor T'ang T'ai Tsung, the founder of the dynasty, and was appointed President of the Board of Works in 630.[16] At about the same time, an Arab mission under Wahb Abi Kabcha reached Ch'ang-an, and in 613 the Nestorian church first introduced Christianity into China.[17] Emperor T'ai Tsung—in accordance with his declaration that "religion has many names; there have been many wise men, and even if their teachings differ, they can be a blessing to mankind"—showed benevolent tolerance towards all foreign religions, and the capital was thronged with foreigners. From this it is not difficult to see who were the "strange peoples" who sat for their portraits by a Chinese painter of the seventh century.

A better known painter, of whom we have not only historical records and vivid description of his works, but also his original pictures, is Yen Li-pen, the younger brother of Yen Li-te. He followed in the footsteps of his elder brother, succeeding him in the Board of Works in 657, and eleven years later becoming one of the two chief Ministers of State. According to the account of the *Ming-hua chi,* Li-pen was in the service of the future Emperor T'ang T'ai Tsung while the latter was still Prince of Ch'in, and in 626 received an order to paint the picture of "The Eighteen Scholars of the Ch'in dynasty," who gathered in the Ch'in palace in 621.[18] In 643 Emperor T'ai Tsung commissioned him to paint portraits of twenty-four meritorious officials for the *Ling-yen ko* (Memorial Hall), portraits for which the emperor himself wrote the

Yen Li-te

Yen Li-pen

63

eulogies. He was also ordered to make pictures of the foreign envoys who came to pay their respects to the Chinese emperor.[19]

Best known among Yen Li-pen's portraits, and a most important document of early Chinese painting, is the large scroll at the Boston Museum bearing the portraits of thirteen **Plate 8** emperors from the Han to Sui. (Plate 8). The origin of this scroll has been ascribed to Yen Li-pen. The best account of its history and a critique of its artistic quality can be read in the article by Mr. K. Tomita in The Bulletin of the Museum of Fine Arts, Boston, February 1932, from which I take the following important points. "The thirteen Kings forming the motifs of the scroll seem to be a more or less arbitrary selection from the long series of emperors of various dynasties who reigned in China, from Chao Wen Ti of the Former Han (179–157 B.C.) to Yang Ti (A.D. 607–617) of the Sui. Among the following five (groups 2–6) we have Emperor Kuang Wu Ti (A.D. 25–27) of the Later Han, Emperor Wen Ti (220–**Plate 9** 226) (Plate 9) of the Wei, Emperor Lieh Ti (Liu Pei) (221–223) of the Minor Han dynasty, Emperor Ta Ti (222–252) of the Wu dynasty, and Emperor Wu Ti (265–290) of the Western Chin, but none of the more remarkable rulers of China during the above mentioned dynasties. Then follow four emperors of the Ch'en dynasty (Nanking 560–589) not in strict chronological order: Hsüan Ti, Wen Ti, Fei Ti, and Hou Chu. The three last figures represent Wu Ti of the Northern Chou dynasty **Plate 10** (561–578) (Plate 10) and Emperors Wen Ti and Yang Ti of the Sui dynasty (581–618)."[20] The scroll is painted in colors on silk. While each group makes a monumental composition by itself, the thirteen figures, shown among their attendants, together form a royal procession. The pictures of the first six emperors are known to have been replaced during the tenth or eleventh century by a far less skilled hand, but the other seven are much older. The scroll is no longer in a condition which can do justice to its original beauty, and in many parts it appears somewhat crude. The figure designs have impressive grandeur. The figures of the emperors, who are drawn much

8 SCROLL OF THE EMPERORS. Attributed to Yen Li-pen. T'ang. Color and ink on silk. Height 51 cm. *(Museum of Fine Arts, Boston.)*

larger than their attendants, are represented as standing in half-profile or moving slowly forward, clad in ample robes with embroidered borders, belts, and head-gear, and the whole picture is executed in a fluent brush line. The well-balanced groups have a touch of unconventional ease, and the main figures reveal some individuality. It is in the figure of Hsüan **Plate II** Ti (Plate 11) of the Ch'en dynasty, though, that facial characterization has reached the highest degree of individualism. The emperor is by no means attractive, but there is a gleam of thoughtfulness in his sharply slit eyes which imparts life to the bloated face. Some arbitrary shading is used with restraint to give volume to the face, but not strongly enough to obscure the important clarity of the brush drawing. To what extent the painter followed earlier models in these portraits is not known, but the interpretations of the various characters are most likely his own. The formality of the ceremonial costumes and the postures are no doubt derived from earlier models. Li Ssu-chen said, "It was the two Yens who made the art of portraiture prosper again after the death of Lu T'an-wei and Hsieh Ho." This scroll shows that he was right.

Wu Tao-tzu Wu Tao-hsün (*circa* 651–716), generally known by his literary title of Wu Tao-tzu, stands above all other Chinese painters. No other artist kindled the imagination of the native critics more than he, yet besides anecdotes and historical data little has been left from which one may judge and distinguish between truth and fiction*. The following story about Wu Tao-tzu's meeting with general P'ei Min is particularly revealing: In the K'ai Yüan era (713–743), at the time of an imperial visit to Lo-yang, Wu was brought there to meet general P'ei Min who offered the painter a quantity of gold and silk if he would draw his portrait. Wu refused to accept the gold and silk and told P'ei Min that he would do the picture only if he would perform his sword-dance to give him inspiration "When Tao-hsüan saw the general performing the sword-dance and observed his life-breath appearing and disappearing, his brush-

---

* It is remarkable that his name is not mentioned in the official history of the T'ang and that his dates are not known.

9   EMPEROR WEN TI. Detail of Plate 8.

10 EMPEROR WU TI. Detail of Plate 8.

work became still more piercingly strong. He did his picture so quickly that it seemed as if a god had helped him. He put in the colors himself, and it became a work of incomparable beauty." It is said that the portrait was a perfect marvel of life and movement.[21]

Among the lesser names of the T'ang dynasty were Wang Wei (699–759) and Han Kan (*circa* 720–760), who are known as painters of landscapes and horses respectively, as well as **Wang Wei** portrait painters. Wang Wei is represented by the Chinese historians as the perfect gentleman-painter to whom painting was but one of many accomplishments—in music, poetry, and calligraphy he attained some degree of perfection. He was born in 699 and later became an official in Shantung. In 756 when the imperial court was scattered and the palaces of the imperial capital sacked by the soldiers of An Lu-shan, Wang Wei was forced by the rebel general to accept the position of censor at his court. As soon as the imperial house was re-established after a few months, he was imprisoned but later released, and regained the favor of the emperor through the influence of his brother, who was popular at court. During the last year or two of his life, Wang Wei was the official in charge of the household of the crown prince; he died in 759.

He mostly painted pictures of religious subject and landscapes with a poetic undercurrent. He made several representations of Vimalakīrti, the legendary ascetic who, according to a popular tradition, had been living in China long before the introduction of Buddhism and who was particularly venerated by the painters for his purity of life and thought. No less than four Vimalakīrti pictures by Wang Wei are mentioned in the catalog of Emperor Hui Tsung's collection.[22]

Another of Wang Wei's portraits represents Fu Sheng **Plate 12** (Plate 12), a famous scholar of the third century B.C. who is said to have preserved certain sections of *Shu Ching* (The Book of History) from the burning of the books under Shih Huang-ti of the Ch'in dynasty. This picture, which is mentioned in the *Hsüan-ho hua-p'u* has been identified with a small hand-

11 EMPEROR HSÜAN TI. Detail of Plate 8.

71

scroll in the Abe Collection at Osaka Museum.* An old man in scant clothing is shown seated on a straw mat at a low table, holding a scroll in one of his thin hands and pointing with the other to a difficult passage. A benevolent smile shows his contentment, and he seems to say that the truth will not be lost. The figure is shown in half-profile, and the table is placed obliquely. Even though the picture is now in a rather decrepit condition, one may still observe the fine ink lines, the light color, and the sensitive execution of the thin face which shows sympathetic and close observation. This picture can be taken as a classic example of the achievements of the T'ang dynasty in the art of figure and portrait painting.

Ch'en Hung

Han Kan, a contemporary of Wang Wei, was also a portrait painter of high order, although his favorite subject was horses. Another painter who excelled in portraits as well as in the painting of horses and buffaloes was Ch'en Hung. He was born in Kuei-chi in Chekiang and must have been little older than Han Kan. We are told that he painted portraits of scholars and ladies and several times was called upon to paint the august countenances of the Emperors Hsüan Tsung and Su Tsung (759–763). Chang Yen-yüan says that "all imperial portraits which he was commissioned to do were the best of the time." His "brush work was vigorous and fluent, his style brilliant and original." According to Chang, he was "the only one after Yen Li-pen."** He was what might be called a character painter, not exactly a portraitist in the modern sense of the word, being an artist who could transmit the character of his models through their types as well as through their gestures, attitudes, and the details of their costumes.[23] Ch'en Hung's style may be seen to some extent in the picture in the Nelson Gallery, Kansas City. It is a short scroll painted in rich colors on silk, which originally represented Eight Meritorious Officials, four civil and four military, but as two military men have been lost, only six figures remain. (Plate 13 shows two of them.) They

Plate 13

* Mr. Taki is skeptical about attributing the work to Wang Wei, believing it to be an early Sung work (See Seiichi Taki, *Fu Sheng*).
** In the *Li-tai ming-hua-chi,* completed in 845.

12 FU SHENG. Attributed to Wang Wei. T'ang. Color and ink on silk. Height 25cm. *(Osaka Museum.)*

are shown in three-quarter view, standing or walking, without any connection between the figures, each one forming a separate picture and personality in spite of the uniformity of their positions. The strong coloring and refined execution of the scroll gives it great decorative beauty. Three colophons have been attached to the picture. The first one is by the well-known painter Wen Chia and is dated 1579; he points out that very few portrait paintings of the T'ang period have been preserved. He is not able to identify the figures. The second one was written by Chang Feng-i, in 1596, who says that Ch'en Hung may be compared with Yen Li-pen. The third colophon is signed by Yüan Yüan, a well-known writer and connoisseur (1764–1849), who examined the picture at the emperor's request; in trying to identify the figures he arrived at no definite conclusions.

Portrait painting during the latter part of the eighth century held a prominent place in court circles. Painters such as Chang Hsüan (*circa* 713–742) and Chou Fang (*circa* 780–810) were kept busy by the emperor and nobles painting portraits, including those of the emperor's favorite concubines, ministers, and strangers from the West, whose exaggerated features have always been a source of delight to the Chinese.

Chang Hsüan, who was nearly fifty years older than Chou Fang (both were active during the latter part of the eighth century), painted landscapes, but according to the *T'ang-ch'ao ming-hua-lu* his favorite subjects were "young nobles, women of rank, and horses." In his day, he was the most celebrated painter of beauty and grace in romantic surroundings.[24] The portrait of Emperor Ming Huang of the T'ang (Plate 14) shows us why. The picture bears no signature, but it is generally accepted as Chang Hsüan's. It shows the emperor playing a flute while lying on a couch, attended by court ladies and two girl singers.

In a note on the artist, T'ang Hou writes, "He excelled in particular in painting young children, in which he was not inferior to Chou Fang," and adds "all married women in his pictures have ears touched with red, by which they are dis-

Chang Hsüan

Plate 14

13   TWO OFFICIALS. Attributed
to Ch'en Hung. T'ang.
Color and ink on silk. *(Nelson Gallery, Kansas City.)*

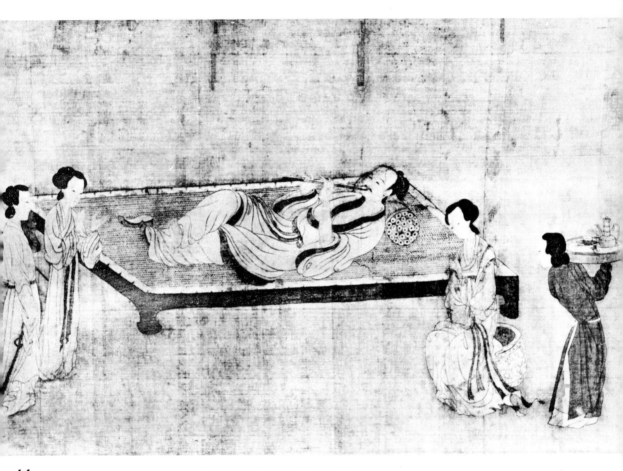

14 EMPEROR MING HUANG. Attributed to Chang Hsüan. T'ang. Color and ink on silk. Height 30 cm. *(Palace Museum, Taiwan.)*

tinguished from the unmarried, who are only touched with red on the lips."[25] Chang Hsüan's best-known work is "Women Preparing Silk," a scroll in the Boston Museum. According to the inscription, this is a copy by Emperor Hui Tsung. It shows T'ang style and the dramatic representation which Chu Ching-hsüan had in mind when he wrote that Chang Hsūan "excelled in rough sketches and in bringing things out with touch."[26]

Chou Fang

Little survives of the secular painting of the time. It is particularly regrettable that none of Chou Fang's famous portrait paintings has survived. He seems to have been a master of psychological characterization, and as such, more akin to Western painters than most Chinese painters of early times.[27] If portrait painting had continued in China along the lines indicated in the art of Chou Fang, it might have led to portraits similar to those of early Renaissance masters. The few fragments of his pictorial art and influence which have survived make us realize that he was a keen observer of human nature. We may see it in two or three examples and in the titles of many of the recorded, but no longer existing, pictures, which can be taken as further evidence of his ability. Chou Fang, who painted at a time when rebellious and aggressive neighbors had broken the hegemony of T'ang rule, was greatly influenced by the destiny of his days. His pictures reveal a heavier mood and more pensive approach to human subjects. Although he had upper class female models, he did not represent them in gay surroundings, but instead isolated against a neutral background. In the *T'ang-ch'ao ming-hua-lu,* Chou Fang is accorded a very high place, next to that of Wu Tao-tzü and above that of Yen Li-pen, and praised as the best portrait painter. Tradition tells us about two portraits of Chao Tsung (Vice-President at the court) painted by Han Kan and Chou Fang, "When Chao Tsung showed both portraits to his wife and asked her to point out the better of the two, she said 'they are both like Mr. Chao, but the first one (Han Kan's) represents merely his outward appearance while the latter (Chou Fang's) transmits his character, Mr. Chao's real nature,

78

the expression of his smile and words.' "[28] In more serious vein are the portraits of Buddhist priests, such as the "Patriarchs of the Chen-yen Sect" series painted by Li Chen.

Li Chen was a contemporary of Chou Fang but has remained practically unknown in China. His name does not appear in any of the old records of the history of painting in his homeland, and he would probably have been completely forgotten were it not for the fact that some of his work was brought to Japan by Kōbō Daishi, the founder of the Shingon sect, on his return from China in 804. The pictures which he brought represent five patriarchs of his sect of Buddhism, the third, fourth, fifth, sixth, and seventh, who helped to establish the new belief in China. These pictures are preserved in the treasury of the Tōji temple in Kyoto, which is the main temple of the Shingon sect in Japan, and some of them include inscriptions attributed to Kōbō Daishi. Besides these five portraits by Li Chen, there are two more portraits to complete the set of seven, but they are inferior in quality and were painted in Japan by an imitator at a later date.[29]

Even though the pictures are damaged—three of them so badly that the figures can hardly be seen—they still leave a strong impression. They are large, 212 cm. × 152 cm., and unadorned, but very dignified. Each one consists of a single figure seated with folded legs in a meditative posture on a low square dais. The uniform design is only in one case supplemented by the addition of a servant, who stands in a reverent attitude at the side of the master. The names of the Chinese and Indian patriarchs are written in large decorative script above or at the side of each figure, and below them broad strips of historical inscriptions are still readable. The third patriarch Vajrabodhi, from South India, reached China in 719 and died there in 732, but the picture of him is hopelessly defaced. This portrait was not made during his lifetime, for Li Chen did not work before 780, nor was that of the fourth patriarch, Subhakara, who arrived in China in 716 and died there at the age of 99 in 735. The fifth patriarch, Amoghavajra, from Northern India, died in China in 774.[29] Since, however,

Li Chen

79

the portraits of the patriarchs must have been posthumous, the question of whether they were based on earlier pictures taken from life, were imaginary portraits, or were actual representations of the sitters' physical appearance is of little significance. In accounts of portraiture in the texts of early Chinese painting, the emphasis is invariably on the painter's ability to present the spirit of the sitter rather than his actual physical appearance, the artist having to project into the painting by a sort of clairvoyance a portrayal of what the man represented rather than what he appeared to be. In religious portraits like these, the effect was gained in part by the painter's drawing of a generalized type rather than an individual; his shaven head, robe, smooth and massive features, and gestures are immediately recognizable as those of a priest. The spiritual quality of such a portrait is also intensified by its resemblance to the formula for portraying the Buddha himself which, of course, was familiar to all. The best preserved of the portraits is the one which represents the Indian monk Amoghavajra **Plates 15, 16** (Pu-k'ung in Chinese) (Plates 15, 16). He is wearing a black cloak and sits on a straw-colored mat on a dais which has ornamented red borders and legs. The colors are not as bright as they were, but with time have become softer in tone. The man who is sitting with his hands on his chest is turned in half profile, like the rest of the figures in the series. The sculptural quality is brought out by the firm drawing— particularly in the bony head and the clasped hands—and by the modeling of the deep mantle folds which are shaded in various grades of black. With these highly restricted pictorial means, the artist has succeeded in creating a picture which reminds us of the best wooden portrait statues preserved in Japan. In two of the other patriarchs' portraits, it is less the main figure than the accessories that can still be seen. The portrait representing Hui Kuo, Kōbō Daishi's teacher, seems to have been exposed to more wear and tear than the others so that the patriarch on the dais can now hardly be traced at all, but the servant in a long white gown who stands reverently at his side is still quite well preserved. In most of these por-

15   AMOGHAVAJRA. By Li Chen. T'ang. Color and ink on silk.
Height 212 cm. *(Toji Temple, Kyoto.)*

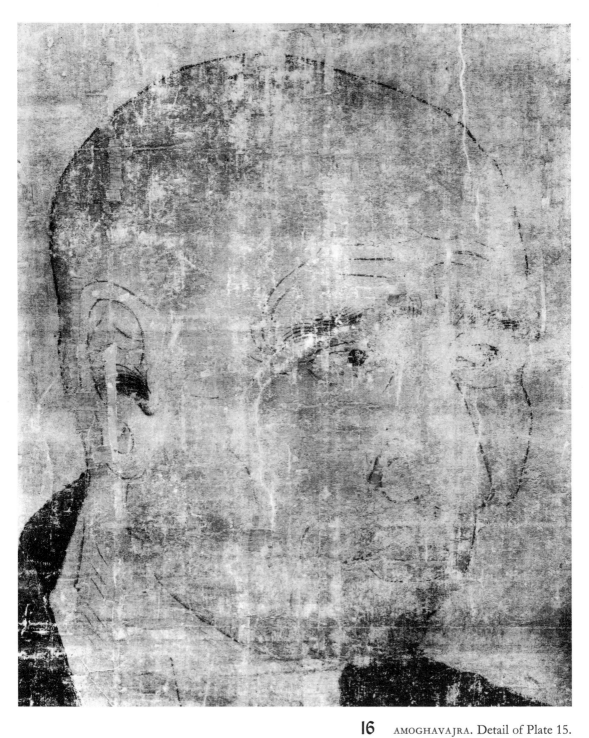

16 AMOGHAVAJRA. Detail of Plate 15.

17 NAGARJUNA. Artist unknown. Japanese copy of T'ang original. Color and ink on silk. Height 213 cm. *(Toji Temple, Kyoto.)*

traits, the slippers or shoes of the patriarchs, placed below the chairs, add some intimacy and serve at the same time to enhance the impression of a third dimension by suggesting depth under the platform.

The portrait of the priest Nagarjuna (Plate 17), from the set of seven, is one of the two which were painted in Japan. It is evident that the painter here followed the manner of Li Chen, but the quality is far inferior. In trying to capture the spirit of the holy man, the painter seems to have emphasized the youthfulness of the sitter rather than his religiosity. According to a legend, Nagarjuna lived five hundred years but always kept his youthful appearance; the painter obviously wanted to capture this aspect. The inscription below the portrait is traditionally believed to have been written by Kōbō Daishi and is dated 821 A.D., fifteen years after his return to Japan.

Plate 17

The historical importance of these portraits can hardly be exaggerated. They are the only ones of their kind still surviving from the T'ang period—the only specimens from a period in which this kind of portrait reached its full development in China.

Li Chen was not one of the leading masters of his time. He lacked both the dynamism of Wu Tao-tzu and the subtlety of Chou Fang. Apparently he was more of a traditionalist, but this does not make his work any less important to us. On the contrary, his work may be said to reflect elements of the T'ang mode of portrait painting at an early stage, when it was characterized by a plastic strength which invites comparison with great sculptures of the same period.

The portrait of the Indian Priest Subhakara (Plate 18) shows a different method which was also used in the portrayal of priests during the T'ang period, based on pure ink-line drawing. The portrait is a part of a hand-scroll which the Japanese priest Ennin, who visited China in 847, took back with him to Japan. The bearded monk seated on a platform is holding an incense burner in his right hand and a rosary in his left.

Plate 18

Defeat abroad and revolt at home brought about the

turning point in the fortunes of the T'ang, and internal collapse was not long delayed. The final disaster was connected with a dramatic personal story which traditional Chinese historians have interpreted as the basic cause of the debacle. In 745 Emperor Hsüan Tsung* took as his favorite the beautiful young consort of one of his sons. This was the infamous Yang

Yang Kuei-fei

Kuei-fei, under whose influence Hsüan Tsung gave himself over to unseemly frivolities. She was painted in a great variety of poses, among the most curious of which must have been "The Lady Yang with the Toothache." Under the portrait, a poet wrote. "Here it was a case of a single tooth, but at Ma-wei, where she was strangled, her whole body ached, and as a consequence of the revolution, attributed to her malign influence, the whole empire ached." She was also painted in the act of mounting a horse, in reference to which a critic pointed out that, whereas the mere act of mounting a horse is always the same, yet it is within the power of the artist to express the different circumstances of each case. Thus it can be seen by the initiated whether the Lady Yang was leisurely mounting her palfrey to the sounds of mirth and songs on her way to the goreo-wood pavilion or whether, as in the present case, she was scrambling into the saddle on her hurried flight to Ma-wei and death.

The Ling-yen Pavilion

In 789 an edict was issued for the formation of a gallery to contain the portraits of all the heroes of the dynasty, from Ch'u Sui-liang (596–658) down to Li Sheng (727–793). Twenty-seven portraits were produced and were hung in the Ling-yen Pavilion, afterwards becoming the subject of a panegyric by a poet named Ts'ui Sung.[31]

In 881 rebellion caused the reigning emperor to flee to Szechwan. When about to return to the capital, he was petitioned to leave behind in a temple "a portrait of his Imperial Countenance." Since the court painters who accompanied his Majesty upon his flight "were all mere brush-holders, incapable of expressing the Divine Features," this gave an oppor-

---

* Known also as Ming Huang.

86

18   SUBHAKARA. Artist unknown. T'ang. Ink on paper. Height 30 cm.
(*Enjoji Temple, Shiga.*)

tunity to a young man, named Ch'ang Chung-yin, who produced a portrait which astounded all the court officials; they declared that "the painter must be a re-incarnation of Chang Seng-yu of old." Ch'ang subsequently became one of the leading artists of his day.[32]

Five Dynasties and Ten Kingdoms

The following fifty-three years are called the period of the Five Dynasties and the Ten Kingdoms (907–960). This is derived from the five short dynasties which followed one another in North China, while in the south, ten kingdoms maintained themselves through all or part of this period.

The original paintings which survive from this period—the years between the fall of the T'ang dynasty and the rise of the "glorious" house of Sung—are not as rare as paintings from the T'ang era, but they are extremely limited in proportion to the numerous painters recorded in the historical chronicles. Kuan Hsiu (832–912) was the only supreme talent of the declining age. His name is traditionally attached to several series of Lohan pictures (Sk. Arhat), among which the so-called

Plate 19

self-portrait of the painter is an exception (Plate 19). The artist felt the need to depict the Lohans more as symbols of hoary age and endless meditation than as human beings. "His sixteen Lohans had bushy eyebrows, large eyes, hanging cheeks, and high noses. They were seated in landscape, leaning against pine-trees and stones. They looked and behaved like Hindus or Indians. When someone asked the painter where he had seen such men, he answered: 'In my dream.' "[33] In the "self portrait" a marked individuality can be noticed. The man's general appearance is Chinese, though the nose is uncommonly prominent and the thick lips are accentuated by a moustache. To support the conclusion that this is a self portrait, we have the inscription on the picture, which is unfortunately in a fragmentary state but was reconstructed by Japanese scholars.[34]

Chou Wen-chü

Chou Wen-chü (*circa* 970), a native of Chüyung, Kwangsi, was an artist of considerable repute who worked at the court in Nanking, which was a center of secular figure painting at the time. His specialty was women, whose faces he painted after the style of Chou Fang, but he surpassed that artist in

19

SELF PORTRAIT. By Kuan Hsiu. Five
Dynasties. Color and ink on silk. Height
91 cm. *(Tokyo National Museum.)*

20

EMPEROR MING HUANG. By Chou
Wen-chü. Five Dynasties. Color
and ink on silk. Height 33 cm.
(National Palace Museum, Taiwan.)

elegance and refinement.[35] The ladies' dresses were painted following a particular method of his own. "The difficulty with women," says a critic, "lies in their characteristic poses ; Chou Fang and Chang Hsüan of the T'ang dynasty, and later on Su Han-ch'en, all managed to capture these perfectly. Success is not attained by rouge and powder nor by ornaments of gold and jade. I remember seeing a picture of a palace lady by Chou Wen-chü. She had stuck her jade flute into her girdle and was looking at her nails, all the while in deep reverie. You could see that she was thinking. It was indeed a marvellous picture." Few painters have reached greater popularity in their lifetime than Chou Wen-chü, whose pictures embodied the taste of the period. His favorite subjects, besides portraits, were of a kind everyone could easily appreciate. The portrait of Emperor **Plate 20** Ming Huang (Plate 20), a part of a hand scroll which in full represents eight figures, is an example of his ability to bring out the spirit of the subject. The scroll, which is executed in flowing brush strokes and soft color texture, shows the emperor and a second chess player sitting at the chessboard. The other figures are two monks, two Taoist priests, one actor, and one court attendant. Although the painting includes many figures, it is the portrait of the emperor which dominates the scene.

5

Development and Stagnation

THE SUNG DYNASTY entered in 960 upon some three hundred years of literary and artistic glory. Under its rule the Chinese intellect seems to have developed along lines which greatly influenced the later periods. It was an era of catalogs, encyclopedias, and voluminous classical commentaries.* In the realm of art, landscape attained its highest point—the names of over eight hundred painters are recorded. The poets of the period wrote their verses with the same brush they used to paint the scene which inspired them. Painting was not a special profession—it was a means by which every cultured man was able to express his thoughts. True artists were also statesmen, men of letters, historians, priests, as well as poets, painters, and musicians. They shunned the fame of professional artists and became known as "gentlemen-painters."

The House of Sung never ruled the whole of China. The beginning of the dynasty was bright and promising, but after a period of centralization and expansion during the reign of Emperor T'ai Tsu (960–975), repeated attacks by the Chin or Jurchen Tartars forced the Chinese to move their capital in 1126 from Kaifeng to Hangchow. The period is thus divided into two parts of almost equal length, known as the Northern Sung (960–1126) and the Southern Sung (1127–1279).

In the encyclopedia, we read the name of T'ung I, who was first and foremost a painter of portraits, the art of which he is

Sung dynasty

T'ung I

* The *T'ai-p'ing yu-lan* published from 977 to 983 under the sponsorship of Emperor T'ai Tsung (976–997), surpassed all previous encyclopedias in volume.

said "to have known at birth." He once introduced into a religious fresco the portrait of a leading statesman of the day, and this was said to have been so beautiful that "it seemed to stand out from the wall." In about 1012 he was painting six frescoes for another nobleman when he suddenly said to his patron, "people nowadays assert that playing the lute is not music and that portrait painting is not art. What is your opinion?" The nobleman drew the artist's attention to a passage in the *Tso Chüan* which stated that lute playing is regarded as music by musicians.

Yen Wen-kuei

We also read the story of Yen Wen-kuei, a landscape painter. He went to the capital seeking his fortune and sold his pictures on the streets. Soon his fame reached the court, and he was commanded by the emperor to paint the portraits of his ministers. When Yen handed over his work, it was found that he had painted instead a portrait of himself. Luckily for him, the emperor could appreciate a joke as well as a painting.[1]

Mou Ku

In 988 a painter called Mou Ku was "dispatched on a mission to paint the portrait of Li Huan, King of Annam, and his principal ministers." He remained in Annam some years, and on his return he was appointed to the Imperial Equipage Department but soon fell into disfavor and resigned. After a few years of retirement, he seized upon the occasion of a visit by Emperor Chen Tsung (997–1022) to a neighboring temple to hang in the doorway a portrait he himself had painted of the founder of the dynasty. When the emperor saw it, he ordered Mou to be brought to him and asked him where he had got the picture. Mou explained that an artist named Wang Ai had been commissioned to paint the founder's portrait, and that when it was finished, another commission for a full-face portrait had been given to him, Mou Ku. Hearing this the emperor rewarded him. Shortly after this incident Mou Ku was appointed to the Han-lin College as the only artist capable of painting full-face portraits.[2]

Wu Tsung-yüan

Wu Tsung-yüan became a professional painter at the age of seventeen and soon made a name for himself by his treatment of Buddhist and Taoist subjects. When painting the thirty-six

Taoist gods on the walls of a temple in Ch'ang-an, he secretly introduced the likeness of Emperor T'ai Tsung (976–997), making his Majesty do duty for a certain red-faced deity, on the grounds that the symbol of the house of Sung was fire. Some years afterwards, the next emperor, Chen Tsung, was visiting the temple when suddenly he caught sight of the portrait. "Why, this is his late Majesty," he cried in alarm, and at once gave orders for incense to be burned while he himself made obeisance before the picture.

Su Shih, also known as Su Tung-p'o, was a great statesman, a poet, philosopher, artist, and a very incisive critic, and his opinions on the art of portrait painting are worth looking at. In one of his notes on portrait paintings, Su Tung-p'o wrote as follows. "The difficulty of giving the true expression to a portrait is with the eyes. Ku K'ai-chih says that the whole difficulty lies in the eyes and that the cheekbones and jaws are of secondary importance. Now on one occasion, noticing that a lamp projected a shadow of my jaw on the wall, I had the shadow outlined, but with no eyebrows or eyes put in. Those who saw it burst out laughing and recognized the likeness at once. If the eyes, cheekbones, and jaws are a good likeness, then the other features will be so too; the eyebrows, nose and mouth can be made like by adding or taking away. If you want to get at the natural expression of a man, you should secretly observe his behavior with other people, but nowadays the subject is made to adjust his hat and clothes and sit down and gaze at some object. How can you expect to reach his real self through such a method? Men keep their thoughts each in some particular spot, such as the eyes and eyebrows, or nose and mouth. Ku K'ai-chih said that by putting three extra hairs on a man's jaw he could bring out his expression at once; he meant of course when the man's thoughts were *in* his jaws. It is enough to portray the spots where the thoughts are manifested, and if painters would only keep this principle in mind, every one of them might be a Ku K'ai-chih or a Lu T'an-wei."[3]

Su Shih adds the following: "When I first saw the portrait

Su Shih

of Duke Tseng, painted by a Buddhist priest who was a friend of mine, I did not think it was a very good likeness, but some days later I went again and found that the artist had come home full of joy. 'I have it,' he cried, and proceeded to add three lines behind the eyebrows, which made the head appear to be looking up, the eyebrows raised, and the forehead wrinkled, thereby securing an excellent likeness."

Ou-yang Hsiu (1007–1072), an eminent statesman and historian, stayed a night at a temple where he discovered the portrait of Wang Yen-chang, a mighty warrior who "could ride at a full gallop brandishing a heavy iron spear which an ordinary man could not lift" and who died in 922 after a life spent almost entirely on the battlefield. His portrait "being almost invisible from neglect and lapse of time, it was handed to an artist to be restored, but not touched up in any way, for fear of losing the likeness." Ou-yang Hsiu was evidently pleased with the results, for he later said, "Already over a hundred years old, it will now last for over a hundred more." We do not know who painted this picture, but to judge from the enthusiasm of such an important man, it must have had merits lacking in later works of the kind.

Li Lung-mien

Li Kung-lin (1040–1106), popularly known as Li Lung-mien, has been described by one critic as "the first among all the painters of the Sung dynasty, equal in brilliance to the masters of olden times."[4] "He was particularly skillful in painting figures. Anyone who looked at them could understand their status in life. Their manners and gestures, their postures, their looking up and looking down, their size and appearance, their beautiful or ugly features were all distinctly marked." Li Lung-mien belonged to a literary family, and in 1070 he himself gained the highest degree in the examinations and began an official career. After serving in several important posts, he was compelled to resign in 1100 because of rheumatism, and retired to the Lung-mien Hill, from which he took his fancy name. He was a man of many talents, "his painting ranked with that of Ku K'ai-chih and Lu T'an-wei, and he was quite without a rival in his day." Like his spiritual ancestor Ku

K'ai-chih, he also painted portraits remarkable for their psychological characterization. One such portrait is mentioned in the *Hua-shih* (an account of painting written by the contemporary Mi Fei) in the following words: "I once saw a portrait of old Hsü Shen, painted in the sketchy manner and animated by a spiritual expression.[5] On it there were three lines of poetry, written in archaic script; the whole thing was an excellent work."* The painter and art-critic Mi Fei also goes into raptures over a group portrait by Li entitled "A Refined Gathering in the West Garden." This work depicted sixteen of the most eminent men of the day, including both the writer and the artist, sitting or standing amid rocks and flowers, dressed in all kinds of fancy costumes; Su Tung-p'o "garbed as a Taoist priest in a yellow robe with a black hat, had just taken his pen to write." His brother Su Che, "resting his right hand on a rock and holding a book in his left, was reading." Li Lung-mien was painting a picture, and Mi Fei, wearing a cap and robe of the T'ang dynasty, was looking upwards and inditing a eulogy of the rocks. . ." "Li Lung-mien's pictures were mostly monochromes and were painted on transparent paper; only in the case of copies of old pictures would he use silk and colors. His brushwork was like clouds passing or water flowing."[6] An authentic secular portrait by Li Lung-mien has not yet been discovered, but we can get an idea of the kind of portraits painted at the time by looking at one small portrait (Plate 21) in an album of full-length portraits of old **Plate 21** scholars, known as "The Five Old Men of Sui-yang", Sui-yang being a district in Honan where these old men lived during the early Sung period. Their names, ranks, and ages are mentioned in the inscriptions, and they seem to have been painted from sketches drawn earlier from life.

The characterization in these portraits depends mainly on the rendering of the white-bearded faces. The scholars are all standing, holding their hands clasped on their chests, and their black gowns and scholar's high black caps are all the

* Probably refers to the *Hsieh-i,* (imaginary portrait), in contrast to the *Kung-pi,* (careful and delicate work).

致仕王渙九十歲郎

21 AN OLD MAN OF SUI-YANG. Artist unknown. Northern Sung. Painting on album leaf. *(Freer Gallery of Art, Washington, D.C.)*

22   VIMALAKIRTI (WEI MO-CH'I). Attributed to Li Lung-mien. Sung. Ink on silk. Height 100 cm. *(Tokyo National Museum.)*

same. But with this utter simplicity in design and color the artist has been able to evoke not only a general air of dignity and thoughtfulness but also individual nuances of character. These men seem to be typical of the Confucian sages who in the Sung dynasty formed the pillars of Chinese social structure. These portraits, typical of the time, represent a tradition that was maintained and developed by Li Lung-mien and his school.

In the *Shih-ku t'ang,* which describes the art collection of Emperors Yung Cheng and Ch'ien Lung of the Ch'ing dynasty, we read of portraits by Li Lung-mien in the collection "The Three Worthies of the Kingdom of Wu" (220–280) and portraits of the Han Emperor Kao Tsu, and five others.

Plate 22

Probably the most important of Li Lung-mien's religious portraits is the one illustrating the Buddhist saint Wei Mo-ch'i (Vimalakīrti) (Plate 22). This hanging scroll is one of the most famous Chinese paintings in Japan. The legendary saint is shown seated in an easy posture on a platform, while a female attendant approaches from the back with flowers in a bowl. The saint has a bearded face with strongly individual features, and his observant eyes are directed on some distant object. His posture, with the raised knee, the turning of the hips, and the draping of the mantle is appropriate to a meditating Bodhisattva. The linear execution, which is soft and fluent, illustrates the style which was popular in China in the twelfth and thirteenth centuries.[*7] It is generally agreed that Li Lung-mien contributed to the development of a new form in his representation of the Kuan-yin Bodhisattva, which in his paintings becomes a suave and graceful lady with strong Chinese features. His picture showing the incarnation of Kuan-yin and the painting attributed to Ho Ch'ung entitled "A Young Lady" support the idea that it was a custom at the time to paint portraits of noble ladies in a form closely resembling that of Kuan-yin, the Goddess of Mercy, the general

* When we compare Li's Vimalakīrti with the portrait of Fu Sheng by Wang Wei, we see development similar to that from Gothic to Renaissance style.

posture being that of the goddess but the face that of the lady portrayed. This is similar to the custom of portraying Buddhist priests in a posture akin to that of the Buddha.

In "Young Lady in White" (Plate 23), sometimes called Kuan-yin, the subject stands half-turned to the right, carrying a basket in her left hand and a fan in her right. The robe which covers her feet is held at the waist with a long sash. The painting is delicate, the design simple, and the noble repose reminds us of a religious painting. It is attributed to a little-known painter called Ho Ch'ung, who was a contemporary of Li Lung-mien. He was a good portrait-painter, and the story is told that while painting the portrait of his friend Su Tung-p'o, the latter asked him, "Why do you paint my portrait?" Ho Ch'ung answered, "Because it amuses me." In the year 1050 he was asked to produce a posthumous portrait of a prominent old baron which on completion was exhibited in the ancestral hall on days of memorial services. This indicates that at least during the Sung period ancestral portraits were sometimes painted by the better artists.

Among other painters who are known to have painted portraits during the Sung period, we find some little-known names.

Chao Tzu-yün is disposed of almost in a line. "He could produce a picture by a single brush-stroke. In painting faces and hands he was careful enough, but would dispose of draperies as if he were calligraphist, in one stroke." He must have worked about 1150.

The famous scholar and philosopher, Chu Hsi (1130–1200), whose interpretations of the classics were obligatory at the public examinations until the fall of the Manchu House, is said to have painted his own portrait, which was engraved at Hui-chou in Anhwei. He also wrote an interesting account of a portrait painted for him by Kuo Kung-ch'en, a well-known artist of the time: "It has always been considered first-class work in portrait painting, even for the most skillful artist, when the result is a more or less exact likeness of the mere features. Such skill is now possessed by Kuo Kung-ch'en, but what is still more marvelous, he catches the very expression

Plate 23

Kuo Kung-ch'en

99

and reproduces, as it were, the inmost mind of his model." Then he adds, "I had already heard much of him from some friends, however on my sending for him he did not make his appearance until this year. Thereupon, a number of the gentlemen of the neighborhood set themselves to test his skill. Sometimes the portrait would be perfect, sometimes perhaps a little less so, but in all cases a marked likeness was attained, and in point of expression of individual character the artist showed powers of a very high order. I myself sat for two portraits, one large and the other small, and it was quite a joke to see how accurately he reproduced my coarse, ugly face and my vulgar, rustic turn of mind, so that even those who had only heard of, but had never seen me, knew at once for whom the portraits were intended. I was just then about to start my travels eastwards to the confines of Shantung, westwards to the turbid waters of the Tun-t'ing lake, and northwards to the home of the old recluse T'ao Yüan-ming, after which I contemplated retirement from public life. And I thought how much I should like to bring back with me portraits of the various great and good, but unknown, men I might be fortunate enough to meet with on my way. But Kuo's parents were old, and he could not venture upon such a long journey, for which I felt very sorry."[8]

Hu Ch'uan, a voluminous writer who died in 1172, writes as follows: "There is no branch of painting as difficult as portraiture. It is not that reproduction of the features is difficult, but the difficulty lies in painting the springs of action hidden in the heart. The face of a great man may resemble that of a mean man, but their hearts will not be alike. Therefore, to paint a likeness which does not exhibit these heart impulses, leaving it an open question whether the sitter is a great or a mean man, is to be unskilled in the art of portraiture."

Plate 24 Liu Sung-mien, a painter of the Sung period, succeeded in capturing this "heart impulse" in his "Nobleman under a Pine Tree" (Plate 24). It is a piece of excellent workmanship; the brushwork is admirable in its variety, treating the figures with the softest possible touch, while painting the pine tree in the

23

YOUNG LADY IN WHITE.
Attributed to Ho Ch'ung.
Sung. Color and ink on silk.
Height 93 cm. *(Freer Gallery
of Art, Washington D.C.)*

101

background in a most vigorous manner. According to Chinese experts, this was painted by Liu Sung-mien, although Japanese experts disagree.

Ch'en Fu-liang, a statesman and writer who died in 1202, mentions a friend's portraits of seven generations of ancestors. "To look upon these faces," Ch'en said, "was like looking at living men."

Yüan Ai   Yüan Ai was a young Buddhist priest who was brought to the capital as a child and subsequently took his vows of priesthood. "He acquainted himself thoroughly with the art of physiognomy and thus became able to draw portraits. The founder of the dynasty, Emperor Tai-tsu, hearing of his fame, sent for him to paint the Imperial likeness. At that moment His Majesty was just back from enjoying the spring in a garden behind the palace. He was wearing a black cap in which some flowers had been stuck, and a joyous expression overspread his face. Almost with a single sweep of his brush, Yüan Ai completed his work. The emperor rewarded him handsomely, and henceforth all the notables struggled to get a picture from him."

When the emperor asked him if he could paint his own portrait Yüan soon produced a picture which His Majesty said was a wonderful likeness. The following story is also told of his skill. "Yüan Ai was on one occasion painting in the Imperial Gallery when the eunuchs who stood round to watch noticed that as soon as he had finished coloring a picture, he would draw forth from his robe a stone which he rubbed over all the flesh. This gave the flesh of the portrait a very natural appearance, such as no other painter could obtain. Once when he had just used the stone, he saw a little eunuch pick it up and run away. He made the boy bring it back, upon which the latter called him several bad names and then disappeared. Since no one could give the name of the boy, Yüan Ai simply drew a likeness of him and went to complain to the official in charge. When he saw the head Yüan had sketched, he recognized the little offender, who soon got his deserts— and Yüan Ai's fame increased by leaps and bounds."[9]

24 NOBLEMAN UNDER A PINE TREE. Attributed to Liu Sung-mien.
Sung. Color and ink on silk. Height 22 cm. *(Private Collection,
Japan.)*

Chang Ssu-kung is completely unknown in China but is highly esteemed in Japan. More than a dozen pictures attributed to him are in Japanese collections, but none of them is signed and no definite dates are known. All these pictures are characterized by an unusual degree of graceful softness and elegance. Besides being a painter of Buddhas and Bodhisattvas, he was also capable of producing excellent portraits, such as the well-known picture of Pu-k'ung (Plate 25). It is a picture of great dignity and decorative beauty. The bearded priest in a red mantle over a violet undergarment is seated in a large chair. His legs, which are crossed on the seat, are hidden by his long robe, and his hands are joined in his lap. He is in the position of meditation, although his eyes are not closed. Due to the excellent drawing, the stout form and the large head stand out in strong relief. This is one of the most convincing and attractive priest-portraits of the Sung period.

Plate 25

Another portrait painted in the same style is the one showing the priest Tao-hsüan-lu-shih, of the T'ang Period (Plate 26). It shows the priest seated in a chair covered with sacred cloth and holding a flapper in his hand. The drawing is wild yet sedate, and the color tones are elegantly beautiful. It is a masterpiece of portraiture. The present work is a copy—the original was brought to Japan from China during the Sung dynasty by Shunjo, founder of Senyuji in Kyoto. It was copied by an anonymous painter during the Kamakura period (1185–1333).

Plate 26

Somewhat later in date, but just as impressive, is the portrait of the famous Ch'an master Wu-chun (1175–1249) (Plate 27). According to the inscription, it was painted in 1238, but there is no indication as to the artist, who may well have been another monk-painter. The style is not very different from that of Plate 25, but the decorative effect is softer. Painters who produced such portraits were primarily concerned with producing objects of worship rather than works of art. They did not sign their names and did not develop individual styles —instead they followed old models for their designs. Wu-chun is seated in a big chair holding his abbot's staff across

Plate 27

25 PU-K'UNG. Attributed to Chang Ssu-kung. Sung. Height 114 cm.
(Kozanji, Kyoto.)

26 TAO-HSÜAN-LU-SHIH. Artist unknown. Kamakura period copy of Sung original. Color on silk. Height 125 cm. *(Private Collection, Japan.)*

his knees. His eyes are wide open, showing intelligence and attentiveness. Wu-chun was one of the most prominent Ch'an masters of the early thirteenth century, active as a writer and painter and also as a teacher, and is known in the history of art as the master of the painter Mu-ch'i. The head shows a great deal of individuality while the body is executed in a much more traditional style, which brings some Japanese scholars to the conclusion that the face was executed by a Chinese artist while the lower part was repainted in Japan by a local artist.

Plate 28

Another portrait typical of the priest-portraits common during the Sung is the one of the Ch'an priest Ch'ing-chao Cheng-teng (Plate 28). Probably painted by another priest, it shows the sitter wearing his official robes. The inscription on the upper part of the hanging scroll is by a priest called Hua-ts'ang and is dated 1198.

In violent rejection of the orthodox soft-line and color-wash technique, the Ch'an painters of the Southern Sung period developed a style using pure black ink with broad brush-strokes. Their paintings, which were inspired by meditative Buddhism, were not created for the sake of beauty, but to express a state of consciousness which could be achieved only after long hours of meditation. The pictures by the Ch'an painters were simple and consisted mainly of landscapes, bamboo, and flowers. Often, however, they portray figures, and strange as it may seem, it was in this apparently simple kind of painting that the artist most often captured the spirit of the sitter, rather than in the soft-line, carefully painted portrait.

Plate 29

The best known representative of this Southern Sung Ch'an painting was Liang K'ai, a successful academician who renounced all official honors and settled in a Ch'an monastery. His works are more appreciated in Japan than in his homeland, and the Chinese historical records about his life and work are incomplete. In his picture of Hui-neng, the sixth Patriarch, tearing a sutra scroll into pieces (Plate 29)—an old Japanese copy of the Chinese original—the speed and strength of the jerky brushwork lifts it to a very high level of

27

WU-CHUN. Artist
unknown. Southern
Sung, 1238 A.D. Color
and ink on silk. Height
125 cm. *(Tofukuji, Kyoto.)*

28 CH'ING-CHAO CHENG-TENG. Artist unknown. Southern Sung, 1198 A.D.
Color on silk. Height 116 cm. *(Shofukuji, Fukuoka.)*

29 HUI-NENG. Attributed to Liang K'ai. Japanese copy of Sung
original. Ink on paper. Height 73 cm. *(Private Collection, Japan.)*

impressionistic ink-painting and suits the posture in which the priest is portrayed. This extraordinary Ch'an master used to greet his students with shouts and roars.

The subtle versatility and great technical skill of Liang K'ai are more apparent in the famous portrait of the poet Li T'ai-po (Plates 30, 31). This picture, which looks so simple, is the best of the painter's works and is considered the ultimate achievement of the abbreviated style of monochrome ink-painting. It reduces to the bare essentials a man in a wide robe which covers him completely from neck to feet, in profile against an empty background. Although there is no realism in the plastic folds or modeling in light and shade, his form is full of grandeur, breadth, and strength. Li T'ai-po is walking slowly, and the proud backward jerk of his neck gives him an air of self-absorbed happiness. The smile on his lips while he is walking and reciting a new poem thus captures fully the spirit of the T'ang poet. From some of the titles of Liang K'ai's works mentioned in the *Sung Yüan-hua lu* we know that he painted several other portraits of poets, philosophers, and various personalities.

Plates 30, 31

Most of the existing Sung portraits are of high priests, with only a few of laymen still known to exist. The portrait of an ancestor of the Sun Family (Plate 32)—probably Wu Kung, the founder of the Wei dynasty—is executed in a typically Sung style. The brushwork is admirably free, and the laying of colors is excellent. The artist is unknown, but the inscription suggests that it was painted at about the end of the Sung period.

Plate 32

Another Sung-period portrait of a layman is that of Pai Lo-t'ien (Plate 33), the Chinese master-poet of the T'ang dynasty. Although the artist is unknown, the work bears an inscription by the priest Wu-hsiao dated 1284, which is likely to have been the year it was painted. Wu-hsiao was the pen-name of Tsu-yüan (1226–1286), a Zen priest who came to Japan in 1280 and founded the Engakuji Temple in Kamakura. This suggests that the portrait was actually painted in Japan by a Kamakura artist who mastered the Sung style. The portrait

Plate 33

30

LI T'AI-PO. By Liang K'ai. Southern Sung. Ink on paper. Height 79 cm. *(Private Collection, Japan.)*

31 LI T'AI-PO. Detail of Plate 30.

has brought out perfectly the poet's grace and suavity, and the artist has cleverly combined different kinds of brushwork.

From 1279 to 1368 the Mongols were masters of China. We do not find any great names in the opening years of the Yüan (or Mongol) dynasty, during which about four hundred artists were active. The first two or three decades of the period were dominated by the traditionalists, who continued to paint in the style of Sung or earlier times with little individual expression of their own.

Ch'ien Hsüan

The best known painter of the Yüan dynasty is Ch'ien Hsüan (*circa* 1235–1290). He came from Wu-hsing, in Chekiang province, and passed the government official examination at the end of the Sung period but did not serve the Yüan court. He spent his life instead as a gentleman-painter. Ch'ien Hsüan was an excellent portrait and figure painter who chose his motifs from religion and ancient history. He was an accomplished master of bringing out delicate shades in the characterization of the figures by expression and movement. This can be seen in his illustration of an episode in the romantic story of Emperor Hsüan Tsung of the T'ang and his fateful beauty Yang Kuei-fei, illustrated in a handscroll formerly in the imperial collection. It represents Yang trying to mount a large horse in order to follow the emperor, who sits on a white horse ready

Plate 34

for a riding tour (Plate 34). Two women servants are lifting the gorgeously dressed lady into the saddle, which is being fastened by a groom, while an older man is holding the horse. The emperor is watching the proceedings attentively, while some servants with tall ceremonial fans and the emperor's bow are standing close by. This illustration seems to reflect a happy and carefree moment in the romantic adventure of Yang Kuei-fei and the emperor. Another picture attributed

Plate 35

to Ch'ien Hsüan is a portrait of a Court Lady (Plate 35) in which the young lady is shown in a long red dress, with a flute stuck in her belt.* (It is known from the records that

---

* It is not agreed whether this portrait represents a man, or a woman in man's clothing. The portrait has been identified by Giles as being of Prince Huan-yeh.

32 ANCESTOR OF THE SUN FAMILY. Artist unknown. Late Sung. Color
and ink on paper. Height 35 cm. *(Private Collection, Japan.)*

33 PAI LO-'TIEN. Artist unknown. Late Sung. Color and ink on silk. Height 104 cm. *(Private Collection, Japan.)*

the painter Chou Wen-chü of the tenth century painted a portrait similar in subject and pose [see page 90].)

Jen Jen-fa (*circa* 1260–1290) attained his artistic fame mainly as a painter of horses, but he also painted figures and landscapes. He served as an official in the Mongol government and held a prominent position as a civil official. His remarkable achievements as a figure painter, and his emphasis on the characterization of his subjects can be appreciated by looking at a large scroll of his which represents Chang Kuo (one of the Eight Taoist Immortals) performing before Emperor Hsüan Tsung the miracle of producing a small horse speeding in the air (Plate 36). The emperor's figure is twice as large as the others in the picture, he sits heavily on his throne, and his face shows the unique expression of a man who, in spite of being a king, cannot understand what he sees.

The colorful portrait of T'ao Yüan-ming (Plate 37), a literary nobleman of the Six Dynasties period (A.D. 220–589), is admirably painted. The subject, who is composing poetry over a cup of wine, is painted in a lively, free style. Although the painter is unknown, the portrait was probably painted at the end of the Sung or the beginning of the Yüan period. The style closely resembles that of the earlier schools but introduces a few new ideas. The brushwork is vigorous, and the coloring—as in the layman portraits of the Sung period—is excellent. T'ao Yuan-ming's inner spirit seems to have been admirably captured by the artist.

Liu Kuan-tao seems to have been a prominent member of this generation, although not exactly a follower of the academic current. He came from Chung-shan in Hopei and called himself Chung-hsien; his main activity belonged to the last quarter of the thirteenth century. In 1279 he was summoned to the court to paint the portrait of Kublai Khan. Among his surviving portrait paintings is one called "Poet at Ease" (Plate 38), in which the subject is reclining on a couch placed in front of a large screen, which is decorated with a picture of a similar scene, while a table and some plants and musical instruments stand at the head of the couch, and two women

Plate 36

Plate 37

Plate 38

118

34 YANG KUEI-FEI (detail). By Ch'ien Hsüan. Late Sung, or Early Yüan. Color and ink on paper. Height 26cm. *(Freer Gallery of Art, Washington, D.C.)*

approach from the opposite side. They seem to have attracted the attention of the man, who is moving his feet restlessly and holding in his hands a fly-whisk and a bamboo stick. The contents of the picture are all displayed with great accuracy and create that atmosphere of summer ease among books and plants so dear to the Chinese scholar, while the portrayal of the figure represents a strictly individual personage.

Like most of the figure painters of the Yüan period, Chang Wu combined his admiration for the old masters with a realistic interest in actual life, and he possessed the power to recharge with his own sentiments and observations the formal patterns which he borrowed from masters of the Sung period He was active in Hangchow around the middle of the fourteenth century and painted mostly in the style known as *pai-miao* (plain drawing) in ink on paper. In this he was following closely in the footsteps of Li Lung-mien. Several of his works are, in fact, free transcriptions of compositions by the Sung master. This can be seen in his excellent illustrations to the *Nine Songs of Ch'u Yüan* which he made in 1346, after the model of Li Lung-mien's ink drawings. These form the ten sections of scroll, each accompanied by a poem, while an

Plate 39 imaginary portrait of Ch'u Yüan (Plate 39), the poet and statesman of the fourth century B.C., forms an introductory picture to the whole scroll. Lu-ts'un has a short note in the *Mo-yüan hui-kuan* about this remarkable scroll illustration. It serves better than any other Sung picture to give an idea of the style of the great Sung masters.[10]

Among a host of minor artists who are known to have painted portraits, we find in the biographies the name of H-li Ho-sun, evidently a Mongol, who was commissioned by Kublai Khan in 1278 to paint a portrait of the great Genghis Khan (also known as Chinggis Khan—his personal name was Temüjin) who had died fifty years earlier. In 1279 he was further ordered to paint a likeness of Mangu Khan, and these two portraits, together with an old portrait of Agotai Khan, were placed in the Han-lin College.

During this period, painters became interested in physical

35

A COURT LADY. Attributed to
Ch'ien Hsüan. Early Yüan.
Color and ink on silk.
Height 87 cm. *(Private
Collection, Japan.)*

36 EMPEROR HSÜAN TSUNG (detail). By Jen Jen-fa. Yüan. Color and ink
on silk. Height 31 cm. *(Hui-hua kuan, Peking.)*

appearance and applied additional modeling to their painting of the face, while painting the drapery in the "broken-ink" manner, with rough sketching. An example of this is the port-

Plate 40

rait of Ch'üan Chung-li (Plate 40), one of the Eight Taoist Immortals. The Immortal is shown holding the Peach of Immortality in his left hand. The painter has succeeded in producing a portrait full of movement and power. The rags which wrap his body signify great age, while the face, with its sharp staring eyes, is that of a man of power. There are several different Chinese accounts of the life of Ch'üan Chung-li, "but all agree that he lived a few thousand years B.C. and that he succeeded in finding the elixir of life."

In the portraits of Confucius by Chao Meng-fu (1254–1322) and the Four Scholars the artists have portrayed the subjects' faces with a care that suggests that the painter had studied the science of physiognomy. Chao Meng-fu was a distinguished

Plate 41

calligrapher and painter. In his portrait of Confucius (Plate 41), he has succeeded in painting a noble and spiritual picture. The whole picture is painted in soft lines, which demonstrate the artist's ability as a calligrapher. The great teacher is wearing

Plate 42

scholar's dress. The portrait of Four Scholars (Plate 42) was painted by an unknown artist who must have had great control and a highly developed brush technique. The lines are flowing, and the faces show individual characters, strongly differing from each other in facial expression and attitude.

37 T'AO YÜAN-MING. Artist unknown. Late Sung or early Yüan. Color on silk. Height 43 cm. *(Private Collection, Japan.)*

38 POET AT EASE (detail). By Liu Kuan-tao. Yüan. Color and ink on silk. Height 34 cm. *(Nelson Gallery, Kansas City.)*

39 CH'U YÜAN. By Chang Wu. Yüan. Ink on paper. *(Wang Collection, New York.)*

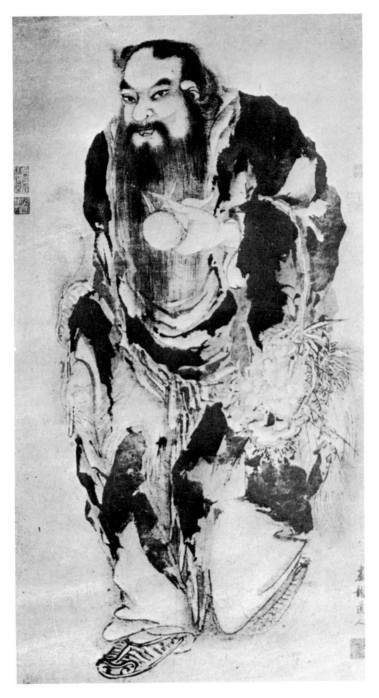

40 CH'ÜAN CHUNG-LI. Artist unknown. Yüan. *(Private Collection, Japan.)*

41　CONFUCIUS. By Chao Meng-fu. Yüan. Color and ink on silk.

42 FOUR SCHOLARS.
Artist unknown.
Yüan. Height
42 cm. *(Cincinnati
Art Museum.)*

6

Decline
and Revival

IN THE YEAR 1368 the first emperor of the Ming dynasty came to the throne, and within a few years the Mongols' last hopes of ruling all China were finally destroyed. The list of Ming painters includes over twelve hundred names. Hung Wu, the founder of the dynasty, was himself a painter of considerable skill with strong convictions on questions of art. There are records of his views on the work of several portrait painters. A sad fate was that of the artist Chao Yüan, who was beheaded when his paintings failed to please the emperor.

Sheh Hsi-yüan and Ch'en Yüan, who both painted portraits of Hung Wu, were more successful in meeting the wishes of their imperial patron. The former was promoted to the position of a government secretary, and the latter became a *taichao* in Wen-yüan ko (painter in waiting, or officer in the Imperial guard). Their paintings of the emperor were by no means flattering, if we may judge by the large full-size portrait signed by Ch'en Yüan which exists in several replicas, of which one used to be in the Peking palace and another in a private collection in Paris. Hung Wu is here characterized with almost repulsive realism—a pock-marked face with an enormous and somewhat contorted chin, large mouth, fierce eyes, and a terrible expression.

The Emperor Ch'eng-tsu, better known by his reign name Yung-lo* (1403–1424), caused the construction of large numbers of new buildings, and many of them were decorated with

* From this period on, we shall call the emperors by the names they gave to the period of their rule.

133

paintings. Artists were called to the capital from all over the country to paint the palace halls. Among these painters was Shang-kuan, best known as a painter of landscapes and birds but also an excellent portrait painter.

Hu Ch'i-pi was "a native of Hai-yen, in Chekiang. He was very skilled at painting portraits and was desirous of painting one thousand portraits of a Buddhist priest called Ch'u Shi, but when about half of these were finished, the priest died. Just then some Japanese arrived, and as soon as they saw one of the portraits, they fell down on their knees and worshiped it, saying, 'This is the portrait of a patriarch in our country.' They next bought as many copies as they could get."

Decline of Buddhism

The decline of Buddhism during this period brought about a decline in the art of portraiture, particularly in the portrayal of Ch'an Buddhist priests, an art which had reached a high standard during the previous Sung and Yüan periods. The gentleman-painters who dominated art at the time looked upon portraiture as an inferior art and left it almost entirely to professionals. Tai Chin, We Wei, and other members of the Che school (named after the birth place of the leading masters of the school, in Chekiang Province) painted many portraits depicting priests, but these painters did not contribute much to the development of the art. One able painter who did not belong to the Che school was Ting Yün-p'eng, who claimed to have rediscovered the painting methods of Wu Tao-tzu of the T'ang and of Li Lung-mien of the Sung; his style, though, was rather rough.

Kuo Hsü (1456–1526) was widely known and esteemed as a figure painter. It is said that pictures of his were worth a hundred pieces of gold. When the foremost painters were summoned to court in the Hung-chih epoch (1488–1505), he was one of those who answered the call and settled in Peking. The only portrait of his which is known to us represents Hsieh An, a very substantial gentleman of the Chin dynasty,

Plate 43

with his three concubines (Plate 43). The picture is executed rather jerkily, and it is difficult to see why this artist should have been so highly appreciated by his contemporaries,

43 HSIEH AN. By Kuo Hsü. Ming, 1526 A.D. Ink on paper.

135

although it is certainly most entertaining as a portrait study.

Ch'iu Ying (1522–1560) was born at T'ai-ts'ang near Shanghai. His pictures are most elegant and full of delicate and graceful detail. The brushwork is so refined that the paintings look as if they have been carved in jade. **Plate 44** The portrait of a scholar beside his lute (Plate 44) is distinguished by its great linear beauty. The surroundings help to establish the character of the scholar, who sits on a low platform as if he is at home, with flowers, wine jars, and a crane symbolizing his natural surroundings. Ch'iu Ying copied the famous works of the T'ang and Sung periods, and so successful were his imitations that they could easily pass as the originals. He was particularly skilled at painting nobles—his men and women were brilliantly colored and looked as if they were alive. "If Chou Fang came back, he could not surpass Ch'iu Ying." His portrait of **Plates 45, 46** Ni Tsan (Plate 45)—probably from the copy by an unknown artist (Plate 46)—painted some time before 1341, when Ni Tsan was still alive, shows his subject seated on a low platform covered by a straw mat, while a boy with a fly-whisk and a maidservant with a water-bottle stand at the sides of the platform. The arrangement is rather formal, and the figures seem a bit stiff, but the picture is significant as a homage to Ni Tsan. The long inscription is a copy of Ni Tsan's epitaph, written by Wen P'eng, in 1542. The picture is painted in pure *pai-miao* technique, drawn with a fine brush in ink, sometimes with a slight addition of color.

Ch'en Hung-shou (1599–1652), a painter who became famous around the end of the Ming, achieved interesting effects by simply ignoring realism and painting portraits in a subjective manner. Like the portraits turned out by members of the Che School, his works frequently border on the grotesque. His first paintings were of flowers, but later he painted portraits. In both cases he displayed more than a passing acquaintance with painting techniques. The portrait painters of this era learned their art by copying old masters, but while they commonly went as far back as Chao Meng-fu and Li Lung-mien, of the eleventh century, few chose earlier artists as models.

44　SCHOLAR BESIDE HIS LUTE. By Ch'iu Ying. Ming.

137

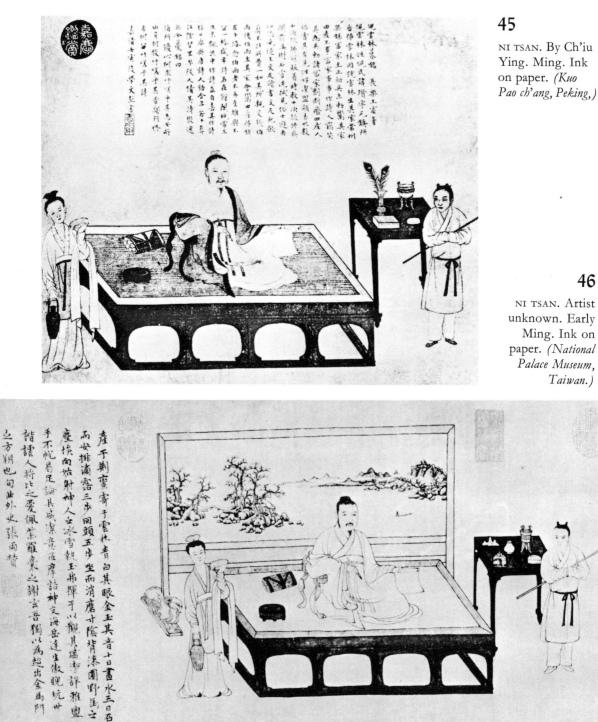

45

NI TSAN. By Ch'iu
Ying. Ming. Ink
on paper. *(Kuo
Pao ch'ang, Peking,)*

46

NI TSAN. Artist
unknown. Early
Ming. Ink on
paper. *(National
Palace Museum,
Taiwan.)*

47

MI FEI BOWING TO THE ROCKS. By
Ch'en Hung-shou. Late Ming. Color
and ink on silk. Height 116 cm.
(Private Collection, Japan.)

Ch'en, however, imitated Wu Tao-tzu and Lu T'an-wei of the T'ang period. Since only a few pictures earlier than those of the Sung and Yüan existed, Ch'en must have relied on stone engravings or on copies. Among Ch'en's works, there are only a few which show T'ang influence. The pictures of the Buddhist Arhats by Kuan Hsiu, of the Five Dynasties period, and a painting of people in a garden, attributed to Han Huang of the T'ang, tally almost perfectly with Ch'en's. The people are heavy and stolid while their clothing is crisp and angular. The thin, wire-like lines are in themselves expressionless. Kuan Hsiu was a follower of Yen Li-pen, and Han Huang was a student of Ku K'ai-chih and Lu T'an-wei. The paintings ascribed to them might well have served as Ch'en's patterns. Ch'en's style was the "studiedly careless"—which was based on Taoist thought, in an effort to destroy the decadent mannerisms of the formalistic imitators of Sung and Yüan art.[2] His purpose may have been worthy, but his portraits are rather staid and ideological. One finds in them none of the warmth and appeal of real human beings. Not only the shapes, but even the lines, are lacking in feeling. It was said that Ch'en's lines show a use of ink that had not been seen for three hundred years, for he emphasized the structural aspect of line and avoided the emotional tendencies visible in most works of the time. This was in fact the style of the ancient past, and it had much in common with the lines found in designs on ancient bronzes and also in paintings of the Six Dynasties and the T'ang. More than anything else he was searching for stability, and he seems to have found it in the ancient world. This was a world not of fickle emotion but of strong will, and that was what Ch'en tried to portray. "Mi Fei Bowing to the Rocks"

Plate 47 (Plate 47) is based on a story to the effect that the painter Mi Fei, who was exceedingly fond of strange-shaped stones, was so impressed by some he saw that he put on his official robes and headdress and paid homage to them as to a man of great rank. The work is more outspoken than is usual with Ch'en. The strokes vary in thickness, and there is a certain emotional strain. The influence of Li Lung-mien or Chao Meng-fu is very evident. This painting is signed "the old and tired one" and presumably was painted in the artist's late years, after the fall of the Ming dynasty.

"Poet Drinking under a Pine Tree" (Plate 48) shows many of the above-mentioned qualities of brushwork. The gentleman-poet is shown relaxing under a monumental pine tree, with a bowl of wine in his right hand. His head is lifted upwards, as if he is in the act of composing a new poem. The self-contained attitude of the figure is emphasized by the carved frame of the pine tree.

Plate 48

In the Ming period, portraits and other pictures of humans were usually painted following standards set in the Sung and Yüan periods, and among the gentlemen-painters there were many who took Li Lung-mien or Chao Meng-fu as their models. They liked to draw in the abbreviated outline (*pai-miao*) style which had come from earlier times and was more illustrative of the Chinese feeling for line, rather than in ink-wash monochrome. In an era when portraiture as a whole was poor, works in the *pai-miao* style fell markedly in quality, despite their glorious tradition. Wen Cheng-ming, Ch'iu Ying, Ch'en Hung-shou, and a few other first rate artists, however, did produce paintings in this outline style that are well worth looking at.

Besides the painters who followed consistently in the footsteps of the ancient masters and did their best to reawaken the stylistic ideals of T'ang and earlier masters, there were others less guided by historical models than by current ideas and actual observation.

Foremost among the latter is Tseng Ch'ing, who lived in Nanking from 1568 to 1650. He was generally accepted as the greatest portrait-painter of the age. In the *Wu-sheng shih-shih* we read, "He painted portraits which looked exactly like reflections of the models in a mirror and grasped the spirit and emotions of the people in a marvellous way. His coloring was refined, and although the figures were simply on paper or silk, their eyes seemed to be moving and following the onlooker as if they were the eyes of real persons. Even Chou Fang, who

Tseng Ch'ing

was known for his portraits, could not surpass him. In his portraits, Tseng gave the noble countenance of the high officials, the refinement of the hermits, the elegance of the ladies, the character of the monks and priests, rendering his subjects' ugly as well as beautiful features in his search for likeness. When you stand in front of his portraits trying to understand them, you forget both the picture and yourself. In painting his portraits, he used several layers of color and worked in a very minute fashion. He walked alone in the forest of art and was known all over the country, which indeed was quite natural." The remark that Tseng Ch'ing worked in a very minute fashion and used several layers of color in his portraits has sometimes been taken as an indication that he was influenced by the European manner of painting, which first became known in China through Matteo Ricci, who reached Peking in 1610. There exists one picture by Tseng Ch'ing which could be said to reveal a Western influence, but it may be worth mentioning that in his notes about Manchu portrait-painting in the *Kuo-ch'ao hua-cheng lu* Chang Keng contrasts the European manner, adopted to some extent by a few painters of the time, with that of Tseng Ch'ing who drew his pictures in ink and was considered a far greater portrait-painter than all succeeding masters, including those who worked in the Western manner. Tseng Ch'ing's portrait paintings were evidently of different class and were much more similar to traditional portraits, not being done simply to serve as symbolic images in connection with ancestral worship but as intimate records of the model's personality and associations. These pictures are not limited to the drawing of the face and the costume; in some cases they also include parts of surrounding landscapes and associated figures.

That portrait-paintings without any landscape are more attractive as character studies (although the painter often used a landscape to emphasize the spirit of the sitter) can be seen in **Plate 49** the pictures of Ch'en Ch'i-ju with a crane (Plate 49) and of Wang Shih-min as a Buddhist disciple (Plate 50); they are both very expressive studies from life, made under different conditions. The old philosopher and art-critic may have been

48 POET UNDER A PINE TREE. Attributed to Ch'en Hung-shou. Late Ming. Color and ink on paper. *(Private Collection, Switzerland.)*

painted on a cold day; he is seated in an armchair wrapped in a wide padded garment, with his feet placed on the rim of a coal brazier which stands between a large wine jar and a crane on one leg. The characterization of this composition is not without a touch of humor, but the gaze of the old man's wide-open eyes is searchingly sad.

Plate 50

The portrait of Wang Shih-min, (1592–1680) (Plate 50), the future great painter, was painted in 1616 when the model was only twenty-five years of age. He is represented as a Buddhist monk-student seated cross-legged on a straw mat, holding a fly-whisk in one hand while the other hand is in a mudra position. A wide garment falls in large sweeping folds around the slender figure, and the head is covered with a cap. His whole appearance is very refined, rendered with lines and light and color wash; only the large eyes, which are staring at the beholder, have a deeper tone. They stand out in contrast to the pale face and add an expression of determination to the youthful image. The Chinese way of rendering the fundamental type of man by means of reducing brush-strokes has here been utilized with perfect success. No wonder the Chinese used to call pictures like this *chuan-shen*—they "transmit the spirit." The art critic Chang Keng remarks, "The best manner of portrait-painting was that of Tseng Ch'ing, who drew his pictures in ink. This was transmitted from man to man, falling finally into the hands of simple artisans who had no real comprehension of it. . . ."

Chang Feng

Chang Feng, born in Nanking, was a scholar who passed the examinations but after the fall of the Ming dynasty renounced his degree, retired completely from public life, and lived in the utmost poverty "in a hut which was hardly large enough to allow him to sit down." The *Kuo-ch'ao hua-cheng lu* contains the following notes about his life and artistic activity: "He was a good painter of landscapes, flowers, and grass and painted according to ideas of his own, which gave him the greatest satisfaction. In handling brush and ink he was like a carefree immortal. He looked very dignified, like a Taoist medicine man from the mountains, and wore a beautiful beard. . . He found satisfaction within himself."[3]

49 CH'EN CH'I-JU. By Tseng Ch'ing. Late Ming.

To judge by these records, he must have been an interesting character as well as an original artist. His surviving pictures, though, do not form a homogeneous whole; some are executed in a highly finished pictorial style, while others are done in a sketchy manner, with a limited number of brush-strokes. In one portrait of the famous patriot and statesman Chu-ko K'ung-ming of the Three Kingdoms period (Plate 51), he shows his characteristic scholarly refinement and concentration on linear beauty and purity. The man, who is wearing a wide mantle and a small cap, is seated in profile, gazing upwards, and can be identified only by the inscription in six large characters, which mean "The late emperor knew that his servant was heedful." From an artistic point of view the main interest is concentrated in the exquisite refinement of the brushwork, which is reduced here to a few essential lines. This is one of the finer outline drawings of the epoch. It has a simple, direct appeal, and the face of the subject is particularly vivid.

Plate 51

The second portrait of the same statesman painted by Chang Feng (Plate 52) shows the subject wearing a similar mantle and headdress. The figure is shown in half-profile, so the facial characteristics can be more clearly recognized. The technique and style in which this portrait is executed stands in strong contrast to the previous portrait. Although neither picture was painted from life, each shows clearly the spirit and character of the gentleman it portrays.

Plate 52

The portrait-painters active at the end of the Ming period were not as numerous as the landscape painters, and those that there were did not contribute to the development of style or to the emergence of new modes or manners of painting to the same extent as the old masters of landscape painting. They remained on the whole more traditional, more firmly settled in the grooves of professional painting. Some of them gained considerable popularity and even fame, yet their painting is not generally placed on the same level as the works by scholars and literati who practised the art of painting as a complement to the art of calligraphy.

50   WANG SHIH-MIN. By Tseng Ch'ing. Late Ming. Color and ink on silk.

This relative estimate of landscape and portrait painting may surprise Westerners, but to the Chinese it was a natural outcome of their attitude to life. According to their view, humans were not essentially superior to other kinds of animate beings, and not necessarily more perfect symbols of the creative forces of universal nature than flowers and birds, trees and stones, mountains and streams. Man became interesting to artists because in his consciousness he could focus the creative thoughts pulsating through visible nature and express them in his actions. Consequently man is usually represented in a significant surrounding which serves to emphasize the character or nature of the model and make the picture more entertaining as a work of art. Such portraits are illustrative records rather than individualized character studies, and this is true too, although for rather different reasons, of the full-size ancestral portraits which were produced in large numbers during the Ming and Ch'ing periods for the purpose of representing prominent ancestors in effigy at the sacrificial ceremonies. Some of these have a special attraction for Westerners because of their characteristic types and decorative designs, but it should be remembered that they were never classified as real works of art by the Chinese. To them, they were merely works of professional skill, painted for the purpose of recording the ancestral heads of the clan.

While the ancestral portraits of the T'ang and Sung periods were of higher quality, softer in color, and with deeper expression on the faces, during the Ming period this art declined. **Plate 53** One ancestral portrait (Plate 53) represents a man who lived during the Ming period. His hat is black, and his robe red. The embroidered panel depicts a phoenix on a green ground, and a large tassel hangs down the side. The chair is draped with a tiger's skin. There is an air of dignity in the figure, coupled with the gentle charm of the face. The smallest detail of the dress—even to the little jade ornaments—is depicted, to the detriment of the portrait, whose object must be that of bringing out the characteristics, which are only to be found in the face and the hands. Even when these are fault-

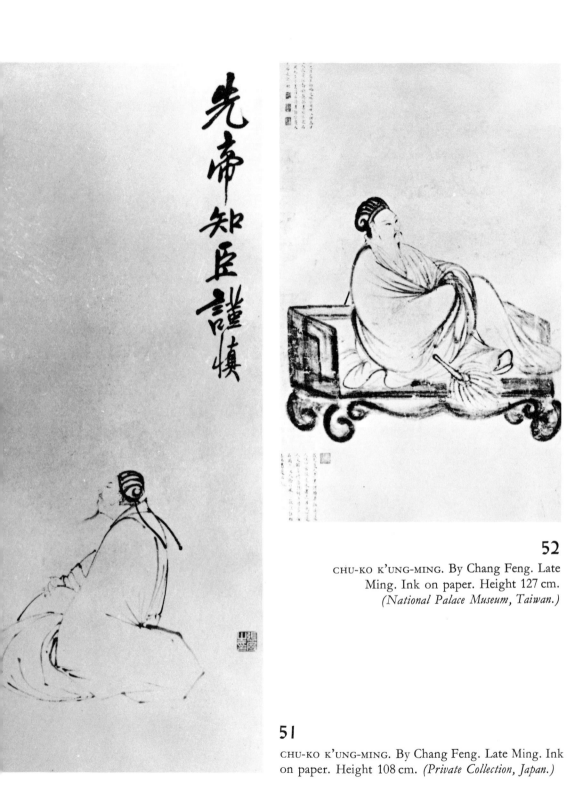

52

CHU-KO K'UNG-MING. By Chang Feng. Late
Ming. Ink on paper. Height 127 cm.
(National Palace Museum, Taiwan.)

51

CHU-KO K'UNG-MING. By Chang Feng. Late Ming. Ink
on paper. Height 108 cm. *(Private Collection, Japan.)*

less, much may be lost in the riot of gorgeous color and unnecessary detail. The more modern the ancestral portrait, the more strongly are these faults accentuated.

Ch'ing dynasty

The house of Ming fell in 1644 before new invaders who came from Manchuria. From the succeeding Ch'ing dynasty came many fine rulers, among them two of the greatest emperors China ever had—K'ang Hsi and Ch'ien Lung.

Nearly a score of painters are mentioned as being attached to the Hua Yüan Palace during the K'ang Hsi period (1662–1722). Among them, Ku Ming and Ku Chien-lung were employed as portrait painters. Ku Ming established his fame by his portrait of the emperor painted in 1671, and Ku Chien-lung became just as famous for his historical portraits. Chang Keng makes the following comment on Ku Chien-lung's work: "Once I saw a picture of his representing T'ang Pin, the governor of the Wu province, which his son considered absolutely like, yet the brush- and ink-work were not free from vulgarity."

Another artist who was allowed to paint portraits of the imperial family—considered a great honor—was Mang K'u-li (1672–1736), a Manchu who served as salt commissioner at Ch'ang-lu, south of Tientsin. Several portraits signed by him were formerly in Peking, and one of them, representing Wang Kuo Ch'in, the seventeenth son of the emperor K'ang Hsi, is at the Nelson Gallery, Kansas City. Chang Keng is no doubt right when he says that Mang K'u-li's manner was based on Western style: "He did not start by making an outline drawing but worked directly in colors. . . The expression of his figures was like that of real people. Those who saw his portraits could not help saying 'This is exactly the man I know.' "

The largest collection of Chinese portraits is now in Taiwan's National Palace Museum, Taichung. In 1949 more than five hundred portraits of emperors, sages, statesmen, and generals were taken from the Manchu Palace to Taiwan, just before the People's Army entered Peking. Some of the portraits in this collection are originals, others are copies—some are even portraits of imaginary persons. None of them is signed, and

53   ANCESTRAL PORTRAIT. Artist unknown. Late Ming. Height 144 cm.

for this reason there is no way of being sure of their date, although they were probably painted during the Sung, Yüan, or Ming dynasties. The six examples reproduced give a clear idea of the techniques of portraying China's emperors at different periods of her history. In each case the face is painted entirely in line and flat tone, yet it is evident that these thin, wiry lines show the features of real individuals. The trappings of power—the imperial robe, the jade tablet, and the headdress—are hardly needed to underline the commanding presence that the portraits evoke.

The force behind these portraits was the hero-cult. Great men had to be remembered by their families, and so their particular virtues had to be recorded for posterity. For this reason, it was important to catch the spirit of the sitter—not merely his physical peculiarities.

Plate 54

The portrait of Emperor Wu Ti (Plate 54), the "Martial Emperor" known as Hsiao Yen, shows him as a gray-bearded man, wearing a crown and holding a jade tablet. The characters on the upper part of the picture give the subject's name in full, Liang Wu Huang Ti. In A.D. 502 Wu Ti seized the throne of the Southern Ch'i and founded his own dynasty—the Liang (A.D. 502–57). He was a great patron of art and literature and a devout Buddhist. His enthusiasm for the new faith was so great that he renounced his throne three times in order to become a member of a holy order, but each time he had to be called back by his government. His portrait shows a man with a devout expression, whose hands are in the position of a Buddhist mudra. Mi Fei, the Sung painter, mentions in his *History of Painting* that he saw a portrait of this emperor, which indicates that early pictures of his were in existence.

Plate 55

Emperor Tai Tsung, the "Grand Ancestor" (Plate 55) known as Li Shih-min, was the founder of the T'ang dynasty and ruled over China from A.D. 627 to 649. His reign is considered the first high point of the T'ang dynasty. He gained power with the sword and was a powerful ruler who killed his two brothers when they conspired to assassinate him; he is known, however, as an emperor who had his people's wel-

54 EMPEROR WU TI. Artist unknown. Date unknown. Color and ink on silk. Height 77 cm. *(National Palace Museum, Taiwan.)*

fare at heart. He crushed internal rebellion, broke the power of China's hereditary foes, reformed the civil and military services, and modified the penal code. He encouraged learning and was beloved by all priests—Buddhist, Taoist, and even Christian—for he allowed Nestorian missionaries to settle in China and was said by them to have had "the grace of a dragon and the beauty of a phoenix." His portrait, which is larger than life size, clearly shows the man's qualities. Appearing stern, he is standing in a yellow robe and wearing a black ceremonial linen hat. He has a girdle around his waist and a pair of black leather boots.

Plate 56
Another good portrait of a warrior is the one of Emperor Chuang Tsung (Plate 56), known as Li Ts'un-hsü, who ruled during the short-lived Later T'ang dynasty (923–925), one of the five dynasties which ruled Northern China one after the other following the collapse of the House of T'ang. Like Tai Tsung, he is wearing a black linen headdress, with a blue robe and a jade girdle. He was one of the many so-called soldier-kings in Chinese history, who came to power at a time of turmoil to reign for a short period only.

Plate 57
Chao K'uang-yin (Plate 57) is known as Emperor T'ai Tsu, the "Grand Progenitor." He founded the Sung dynasty and ruled China from 960 to 975. Descended from a family of officials, he rose to high military command in the Later Chou dynasty. The disturbed state of the empire gave him his chance to gain full authority. He was fond of study and impressed the need for it even on military officers. He himself chose his officials, and let them remain in office for long periods if they showed themselves to be able. In every war he fought, his order was that there should be neither slaughter nor looting. In this portrait he is shown seated on his throne wearing a formal headdress, a yellow robe, and a red girdle. His face shows kindness and sympathy.

Plate 58
Emperor Shih Tsu, the "Regenerating Progenitor" (Plate 58), is the Chinese name of the Tartar Kublai Khan, the grandson of Genghis Khan. He became the ruler of China in 1260 and ruled for thirty-four years. During his reign Peking was

154

55

EMPEROR T'AI TSUNG. Artist
unknown. Date unknown.
Color and ink on silk.
Height 271 cm. *(National
Palace Museum, Taiwan.)*

155

56

EMPEROR CHUANG TSUNG.
Artist unknown. Date
unknown. Color and ink
on silk. Height 272 cm.
(National Palace Museum,
Taiwan.)

157

57 EMPEROR T'AI TSU. Artist unknown. Date unknown. Color and ink on silk. Height 191 cm. *(National Palace Museum, Taiwan.)*

58 KUBLAI KHAN—THE EMPEROR SHIH TSU. Artist unknown. Date unknown. Color and ink on silk. Height 59 cm. *(National Palace Museum, Taiwan.)*

one of the most important cities in the world. In 1276 his forces crushed the Southern Sung and brought the whole of China under Tartar rule. Although he was not himself Chinese, he was accepted as the emperor of a Chinese dynasty and was an enlightened ruler. Marco Polo, who visited the Chinese court during Shih Tsu's reign, was greatly impressed by the "magnificence of the Great Khan, the cosmopolitan nature of his empire, and the wealth and civilization of China." Although conquest was the Tartar way of life, Kublai Khan is portrayed with the features more of a scholar than of a warrior.

Plate 59

Empress Ma Hou (1332–1282) (Plate 59) was the wife of Emperor T'ai Tsu, the founder of the Ming dynasty. She is known as a kind and wise woman who was a devoted wife and very fond of reading. She would not allow her relatives to receive official honors. She strove to moderate the passionate temper of her husband, and when he asked her, on her deathbed, for her last wish, she replied, "That your Majesty would strive for what is good, accept reproof, and be as careful at the end as at the beginning."

How closely these six portraits resemble the physical features of the rulers is of little importance. Whenever they were painted, it was still during the phase of art when the painting of portraits was primarily didactic and their main function was to illustrate examples of ethical behavior and to capture the spirit. "It is not the beauty of the figure but the beauty of the moral that is important" was the theme of Chinese portrait painting during the early period of its development.

59 EMPRESS MA HOU. Artist unknown. Date unknown. Color and ink on silk. Height
66 cm. *(National Palace Museum, Taiwan.)*

7
Western
Influence

THE MAN WHO first brought knowledge of the European way of painting, with its use of light and shade, was the first Jesuit missionary to China, Matteo Ricci (1552–1610) who arrived in 1572. He was not a painter himself but he did possess some knowledge of the art. He brought with him several pictures and religious engravings, which were soon to excite much curiosity among the Chinese. One person, having seen European pictures of Christ, Mary, and the saints wrote, "They are just like images in a mirror and look as though they could move by themselves. They have a magic beauty that Chinese artists could never achieve." Another commented, "These portraits have natural perspective, and there are lights and darks in the houses. How wonderful the Westerners are!" Many others also praised the exotic paintings, and their enthusiasm is understandable, considering the poor state of Ming portraiture, of which Matteo Ricci had the following criticism: "The paintings of China show only the light and do not show the shadows. The faces of people in portraits are flat and shallow." During earlier periods, in particular the T'ang period, realism had enjoyed a certain vogue, but the technique had gradually been abandoned, and during the Ming period only a trace of it remained.

Having recovered from the initial shock of seeing the Christian portraits, a number of Ming artists—for the most part professional—set out to learn Western methods. The men of letters were still too absorbed with the past to adopt anything so new, and while many of them expressed admiration for

Christian art

163

Western art, they made no positive attempt to imitate it. On the other hand, the professional painters, who belonged to a lower class, were not as troubled by the necessity of preserving traditional culture, and a number of them who specialized in portraiture recognized the many advantages of Western realism.

Tseng Ch'ing

In several modern works on art published in China, it is stated that the first Chinese to use Western techniques was the late-Ming portraitist Tseng Ch'ing. He was a native of Fukien but lived in Nanking, where he founded the *P'o-ch'en* school. He had many followers, some even during the Ch'ing period. The following appraisal of him was made by a contemporary: "He has grasped the spirit of the subject so completely that his painting is like a reflection in a mirror. There is moist softness in his coloring, and the eyes glitter. They are only paintings, but they are so close to reality that the subjects seem to be alive." Of Tseng's technique it was said, "He uses as many as ten levels of shading, and his workmanship is very thorough." To judge from this, Tseng must have used perspective and attempted in every way to be realistic. Tseng Ch'ing was the founder of a school that emphasized line, as opposed to coloring, and this was a very traditional approach. One person described his work as follows: "He first draws the framework in ink and then adds coloring. When he paints the face, the spirit of the subject is present in the ink lines themselves." There is nothing Western about this. The problem then is to determine just how Tseng combined line and color. His color portraits resemble some of the Ming ancestral portraits in which the head is strikingly characterized, though rendered almost entirely with lines and no shadows, while the costume is painted with layers of colors and sometimes ornamented. Like the Ming portraits, Tseng's are rarely signed and are usually considered by the Chinese as ancestral images alone, and not as works of art. Yet the best among them reveal a degree of individual character and decorative beauty which makes them interesting as works of art.

Plate 60

Tseng Ch'ing's portrait of Su Tung-p'o (Plate 60) was

164

painted in 1641, when Tseng Ch'ing was seventy-four. Su is the most highly esteemed writer in Chinese history, and Tseng probably regarded him very highly. The artist's attention is focused on the face, and the clothing is treated rather perfunctorily. There are realistic shadows. The general effect is lifelike enough to have made people of the age say that it "appeared to be alive," but the clothing is another matter. The lines that compose it have the same severely archaic quality that can be seen in the work of Ch'en Huang-shou (1599–1652). This painting suggests that Tseng considered line and color as two separate entities. The almost tactile rendering of the face, however, must have been revolutionary at the time, when shading had virtually passed out of existence. The question remains, however, whether this resulted from Western influence or not. It is probable that Tseng had an opportunity to see Christian paintings when Ricci visited Nanking in 1595 and 1599. Furthermore, he is known to have used a substance called "western red" which was an animal pigment introduced by Ricci. It is certain, then, that his lifelike treatment of the face was influenced by Western ideas of shading, although he was not fully converted to the Western style. As seen in this picture, he used shading only on the face and painted the clothes and other objects in traditional style. Tseng subordinated Western elements to Chinese elements in this painting, no doubt because he was faithful to the tradition of linear art.

Other late seventeenth-century painters who tried to form a new style by linear perspective and plastic modeling were Chiao P'ing-chen and Leng Mei, both of whom were particularly well-known for their portraits because they gave very flattering likenesses of the sitters.

In the work of other portrait painters who used a decorative style the Western influence is clearly marked, but sometimes the picture has been softened to the more graceful linear form so loved by the Chinese.

Yü Chih-ting (1647–1705) is regarded by the Chinese as a great master of portrait painting. In describing his artistic accomplishments Chang Keng writes "His portraits were mostly

Yü Chih-ting

executed in the *pai-miao* technique, though he did not follow the style of Li Lung-mien, but imitated Wu Tao-tzu's style." (The reference to Wu Tao-tzu's technique refers to the long wavy folds in the garments of some of his figures.)

Plate 61

Yü Chih-ting's group portrait of five scholars meeting on a garden terrace after an absence of twenty years (Plate 61) is a masterpiece of outline drawing. It is not only a faithful illustration of types and mood but also a characterized illustration of the models as well. The figures have a realism which is clearly a result of Western influence, yet the painter has used —as he did with most of his works—Chinese techniques, which contributed to his popularity among his countrymen, who considered him the greatest master of portrait painting.

Plate 62

Western elements can also be seen in the portraits by unknown artists which were so popular in China during this period. "A Monk" (Plate 62) is reminiscent of the Portraits of the Emperors scroll of Yen Li-pen (see Plate 8). The Western principles in the modeling of the face, however, are quite obvious. One's first impression of the monk is of a kindly man of strong character and self discipline. The face shows intellect, and the hands holding a rosary reveal keen sensitivity.

Plate 63

"Scholar Dressed for Fishing" (Plate 63) is a delightful monochrome portrait of a fisherman, painted in a remarkable ink wash. The artist shows an unusually attractive fisherman who, although his clothes are ragged and his whole appearance poor, yet has a smile on his face and a humorous twinkle in his eye. He seems to be a philosopher, a fact which might support the idea that the fisherman portrayed here is actually a man of high rank who, in accordance with the Taoist philosophy, gave away all his wordly possessions to live in harmony with nature.

Plate 64

"An Old Man" (Plate 64) by Hwang Ying-p'iao, an obscure painter of the Ch'ing, is another work in which Chinese traditional elements have been wonderfully combined with Western ideas. The white beard and bushy eyebrows of this old man make us feel respect for him, while the merry look

栗文忠公採芝圖

辛己仲夏之吉

淺里曾熙故繪

60

SU TUNG-P'O. By Tseng
Ch'ing. Ming, 1941 A.D.
Color and ink on silk.
Height 115 cm. *(Private
Collection, Japan.)*

61   FIVE SCHOLARS. By Yü Chih-ting. Ch'ing. Color and ink on silk. Height 37 cm. *(Private Collection, China.)*

62 A MONK. Artist unknown. Late Ming or Ch'ing. Color and ink on silk. Height 34 cm. *(Private Collection, China.)*

63 SCHOLAR DRESSED FOR FISHING. Artist unknown. Ch'ing. Ink on silk. Height 42 cm. *(Private Collection, China.)*

64   AN OLD MAN. Attributed to Hwang Ying-p'iao. Ch'ing. Color and ink on silk. Height 160 cm. *(Private Collection, China.)*

in his eyes and his pleasant smile make him a real Santa Claus. He seems to be guarding the fruit and flowers in the basket as if they were treasures. The strong realism and the elements of shading indicate that the artist worked under strong Western influence. The inscription on the other part of the portrait gives us a further insight into his personality. It reads:

> I have seen the clouds and mists everywhere under heaven,
> I have always spoken sincerely, but not disparaged other men,
> Poverty has often compelled me to wear straw sandals while traveling,
> But I have been satisfied to gather beautiful flowers from all parts of the world.

*   *   *

The conclusion of the book at this point is by no means an indication that nothing significant occurred in the development of portrait painting in China during the last two and a half centuries. During the eighteenth century the European influence dominated Chinese art. European prints which were sent from Europe were copied by the Chinese with varying degrees of success. "A case of prints after Poussin, Mignard" is listed among the goods sent from France in the ship *Amphitrite*, and a writer in 1804 states that the "colored prints of Europe that are carried out to Canton are copied there with the most wonderful fidelity." Among these copies were many portraits of European personalities, but since the copyists were consciously imitating in technique and subject matter the European originals, without any Chinese feeling, they can hardly be classified as Chinese portraits. Such is the portrait

Plate 65 of Martin Luther painted on a vase (Plate 65) (the companion to which is decorated with a portrait of Calvin.)

Plate 66 A further illustration is the portrait of Chang-tung (Plate 66), the well-known viceroy and scholar who died at the beginning of this century. It is not painted but is made by the weaving together of threads of black and white silk. The work must not be mistaken for embroidery, for no needle has been

65

MARTIN LUTHER. Artist unknown. Ch'ing. Monochrome ink on porcelain vase. Height 18 cm.
(Private Collection, England.)

66

CHANG-TUNG. Artist unknown. Late Ch'ing. Woven
silk. Height 34 cm. *(Private Collection, China.)*

used, and when the hand is passed over the surface of the portrait, nothing is felt but the smooth texture of the silk. The light and dark shades are admirably rendered, and even the gray hairs of the beard are most lifelike.

Portraiture in China today

Since the People's Government came to power in 1950, the heavy seriousness of the centralized government has influenced the development of the arts. The personality cult so strongly practiced by the rulers of New China has encouraged interest in the personality of individual men, thus stimulating realistic portraiture.

Most of the new portraits are frankly propagandist, taking their character from Russian proletarian realism. This new, realistic attitude toward portrait painting is bound to continue for some years to come, but if we remember the strong sense of history and pride in tradition which has been an inherent Chinese trait in all phases of their long history, we may conclude that the time will come when once again idealistic and spiritual portraits will gain a prominent place in Chinese art.

List of Dynasties
Sources
Bibliography
Index

Shang-yin	1766–1122 B.C.	
Chou	1030–256	WESTERN CHOU *c. 1050–770 B.C.* SPRING AND AUTUMN PERIOD *722–481* WARRING STATES *481–221*
Ch'in	221–206	
Han	206 B.C.–A.D. 220	FORMER HAN (WESTERN) *206 B.C.–A.D. 8* HSIN *8–25* LATER HAN (EASTERN) *25–220*
Three Kingdoms	221–280	SHU-HAN *220–63* WEI *220–65* WU *222–80*
Southern (Six) Dynasties	265–589	CHIN (WESTERN) *265–317* CHIN (EASTERN) *317–420* LIU SUNG *420–78* SOUTHERN CH'I *478–502* LIANG *502–57* CH'EN *557–89*
Northern Dynasties	386–581	NORTHERN WEI *386–535* EASTERN WEI *534–43* WESTERN WEI *535–57* NORTHERN CH'I *550–77* NORTHERN CHOU *557–81*
Sui	581–618	
T'ang	618–906	
Five Dynasties	907–960	LATER LIANG *907–22* LATER T'ANG *923–36* LATER CHIN *936–48* LATER HAN *946–50* LATER CHOU *951–60* LIAO *907–1125* HSI HSIA *990–1227*
Sung	960–1279	NORTHERN SUNG *960–1126* SOUTHERN SUNG *1127–1279*
Yüan	1279–1368	CHIN *1115–1234*
Ming	1368–1644	
Ch'ing	1644–1912	
Republic	1912–	

Sources

Chapter 2

1. William Cohn, *Ostasiatische Portraitmalerei*. See also Serge Elis-séeff, *Notes sur le Portrait en Extrême-Orient*

Chapter 3

1. Translated by Giles, Waley, Hackney and Bushell
2. S. W. Bushell, *Chinese Art,* Vol. II
3. Mario Prodan, *Chinese Art,* p. 146
4. Bushell, *op. cit.*
5. Herbert Giles, *An Introduction to the History of Chinese Pictorial Art,* p. 2
6. *Ibid.,* p. 4
7. Bushell, *op. cit.* p. 119
8. *Encyclopedia of World Art,* Vol. III, p. 495
9. Bushell, *op. cit.,* p. 119
10. Giles, *op. cit.,* p. 9
11. *Ibid.,* p. 8
12. *Ibid.,* p. 9
13. *Ibid.,* p. 10
14. Richard C. Rudolph and Wen Yu, *Han Tomb Art of West China,* Plates 44, 45, 64, 65
15. Kodansha, *Sekai Bijitsu Taikei: Chūgoku-Bijutsu,* Vol. I
16. Hamada Kōsaka, *On Chinese Painting in the Han Period.* See also Kōsaka's *On the Painting of the Han Dynasty,* and Osvald Sirèn's *Chinese Painting: Leading Masters and Principles,* Vol. I, p. 24

Chapter 4

1. Giles, *op. cit.,* p. 15
2. Burlington Magazine, *Ku K'ai-chih.* See also Sirèn, *op. cit.,* Vol. I, pp. 26–35, Arthur Waley's *An Introduction to the Study of Chinese Painting,* pp. 45–48, Giles, *op. cit.,* pp. 18–21, and Bushell, *op. cit.,* p. 122
3. Giles, *op. cit.,* p. 18
4. Waley, *op. cit.,* p. 47
5. *Ibid.,* p. 48
6. Giles, *op. cit.,* p. 18
7. Bushell, *op. cit.,* p. 121
8. *Ibid.,* p. 123. See also Giles, *op. cit.,* p. 24
9. Giles, *op. cit.,* p. 28
10. Sirèn, *op. cit.,* Vol. I, p. 46
11. Arthur Waley, *The Rarity of Ancient Chinese Paintings*
12. Sirèn, *op. cit.,* Vol. I, p. 53
13. Kodansha, *op. cit.*
14. Chosen Government-General, *Chosen Koseki Zufu,* Vol. II
15. Bushell, *op. cit.,* p. 126
16. *Li-tai ming-hua chi,* Chap. IX
17. Giles, *op. cit.,* p. 40
18. *Ibid.,* p. 40
19. Sirèn, *op. cit.,* Vol. I, p. 97
20. Kojiro Tomita, *Portraits of the Emperors by Yen Li-pen*
21. Sirèn, *op. cit.,* Vol. I, p. 110
22. *Ibid.,* pp. 125–134.
23. Sirèn, *op. cit.,* Vol. I, p. 140
24. Alexander Soper (trans.), *T'ang-ch'uo ming-hua-lu*
25. Giles (trans.), *Hua Chien*
26. Soper, *op. cit.*
27. William Cohn, *Chinese Painting,* p. 54
28. Sirèn, *op. cit.,* p. 146. See also Giles, *op. cit.,* pp. 71, 72. The story is repeated in the *T'u-hua chien-wen chih*
29. Bijutsu Kenkyu, *Seven Founders of the Buddhism*
30. Waley, *op. cit.,* p. 159
31. Giles, *op. cit.,* p. 69
32. *Ibid.,* p. 76
33. Described by Huang Hsiu-fu in the *I-chou ming-hua lu*
34. T. Akiyama, *Kuan-hsih Self-Portrait,* p. 391
35. *Hsuan-ho hua-p'u,* Vol. VII
36. Giles (trans.), *Hua Chien,* pp. 7, 8

Chapter 5

1. Giles, *op. cit.,* p. 106
2. *Ibid.,* pp. 108, 109
3. *Ibid.,* p. 120
4. A. E. Myer, *Chinese Paintings as Reflected in the Thought and Art of Li Lung-mien*
5. Sirèn, *op. cit.,* Vol. II, pp. 50, 51
6. Giles, *op. cit.,* p. 125
7. William Cohn, *Chinese Painting*
8. Giles, *op. cit.,* p. 142
9. *Ibid.,* p. 151
10. Kojiro Tomita, *The Nine Songs of Ch'u Yuan.* Mr. Tomita gives a translation of the texts which accompany the painting on the scroll

Chapter 6

1. Giles, *op. cit.,* p. 175
2. Yoshiho Yonezawa, *Painting in the Ming Dynasty,* p. 41
3. Sirèn, *op. cit.,* Vol. V, p. 140

Chapter 7

1. Yonezawa, *op. cit.,* p. 43
2. J. Barrow, *Travels in China,* p. 327

Bibliography

Akiyama, T.: *Kuan-hsih Self Portrait,* Bijitsu Ronko

Barrow, J.: *Travels in China,* 1804

Bijutsu Kenkyu: *Seven Founders of the Shingon Buddhism,* 1955

Burlington Magazine ; "Ku K'ai-chih," London, 1904

Bushell, S. W.: *Chinese Art,* Vol. II, London 1906

Cahill, J.: *Chinese Painting,* Cleveland, Ohio, 1960

Chosen Government-General: *Chosen Koseki Zufu* (Album of Korean Antiquities), Volume II, Seoul, 1920

Cohn, William: *Chinese Painting,* London, 1948

——: *Ostasiatische Portraitmalerei,* 1923

Creel, Herrlee G.: *The Birth of China,* New York, 1954

Elisséeff, Serge: *Notes sur le Portrait en Extrême-Orient,* Paris, 1922

Encyclopedia of World Art, Vol. III, New York, 1961

Ferguson, J. C.: *Chinese Painting,* Chicago, 1927

——: (trans.): *Li Tai Chu Hua Mu* (Index of Recorded Paintings), Nanking, 1933

——: *Outlines of Chinese Art,* Chicago, 1918

Fitzgerald, Charles P.: *China, A Short Cultural History,* New York 1962

Giles, Herbert: *A Chinese Biographical Dictionary,* New York, 1964

——: (trans.): *Hua Chien*

——: *An Introduction to the History of Chinese Pictorial Art,* Shanghai, 1918

Hackney, L. W.: *Guide-Posts to Chinese Painting,* New York, 1927

Heibonsha: *Sekai Bijutsu Zenshu,* Volumes 7, 8, 14, 20, Tokyo, 1962

Hirth, Friedrich: *Native Sources for the Study of Chinese Pictorial Art,* New York, 1917

Kadokawa, *Sekai Bijutsu Zenshu,* Volumes 12–17. Tokyo 1963

Kodansha: *Sekai Bijutsu Taikei: Chūgoku-Bijutsu,* Volume 1, Tokyo, 1962

Kōsaka, Hamada: *On Chinese Painting in the Han Period,* Kokka No. 508, 509

Kōsaka, Hamada: *On the Painting of the Han Dynasty,* Memoirs of the Research Department of the Toyo Bunko, No. 8, Tokyo, 1936

Myer, A. E.: *Chinese Painting as Reflected in the Thought and Art of Li Lung-mien,* New York, 1923

Otsuka Kogeisha: *The Pageant of Chinese Painting,* (Shina Meiga Hokan), Tokyo, 1936

Prodan, Mario: *Chinese Art,* New York, 1958

Reischauer, Edwin O. and Fairbank, John K.: *East Asia* : *The Great Tradition,* Tokyo, 1962

Rowley, George: *Principles of Chinese Painting,* Princeton, 1959

Rudolph, Richard C., and Wen Yu: *Han Tomb Art of West China,* Berkeley, Calif., 1951

Saito, R.: *Biographical Dictionary of Chinese Painters,* Volumes 1–4, Tokyo, 1900

Shimada, Shūjirō and Yonezawa, Yoshiho: *Paintings of the Sung and Yuan Dynasties,* Tokyo 1952

Sickman, Laurence, and Soper, Alexander: *The Art and Architecture of China,* London, 1956

Sirèn, Osvald: *The Chinese on the Art of Painting,* New York, 1963

——: Chinese Painting: *Leading Masters and Principles* Volumes 1–7: London, 1956

Soame, J. R.: *Chinese Export Art in the Eighteenth Century,* London, 1950

Soper, Alexander (trans.): *T'ang-ch'uo ming-hua lu*

Strehlneek: *Chinese Pictorial Art,* Shanghai, 1914

Taki, Seiichi: *Fu-sheng,* Kokka No. 588

Tomita, Kojiro: *The Nine Songs of Ch'u Yuan,* Bulletin of the Museum of Fine Arts, Number 35, Boston, 1937

——: *Portraits of the Emperors by Yen Li-pen,* Bulletin of the Museum of Fine Arts, Number 30, Boston, 1930

Waley, Arthur: *An Index of Chinese Artists,* London, 1922

——: *An Introduction to the Study of Chinese Painting,* London, 1923

——: *The Rarity of Ancient Chinese Paintings, Burlington Magazine* Number 171, London

Werner, E. T. C.: A Dictionary of Chinese Mythology, New York, 1961

Yonezawa, Yoshiho: *Painting in the Ming Dynasty,* Tokyo, 1956

Index